Praise for Go Be Kind

"**Go Be Kind** is a light-hearted journal with a sharp-minded message: If you feel something's missing in your life, kindness might be the prescription. This book will guide you through exercises to increase your kindness quotient and will take you on an adventure that will definitely change your life and might even change the world."

—DANIEL H. PINK, AUTHOR OF *WHEN* AND *DRIVE*

"An absolute gem. **Go Be Kind** is not just a manifesto for making life—and ourselves—better, happier and more connected, but sends readers on kindness adventures out in the world and deep into the soul to figure out how. Utterly delightful."

—BRIGID SCHULTE, AWARD-WINNING JOURNALIST, AUTHOR OF THE *NEW YORK TIMES* BESTSELLING *OVERWHELMED: WORK, LOVE, AND PLAY WHEN NO ONE HAS THE TIME*, AND DIRECTOR OF THE BETTER LIFE LAB AT NEW AMERICA

"Leon is the real deal. What he created with this little journal, changed his life and can change yours too!"

—TED KLONTZ, COAUTHOR OF *THE FINANCIAL WISDOM OF EBENEZER SCROOGE*

"A meaningful read? A heartwarming book? Yes and yes—and so much more. **Go Be Kind** is an experience, a pathway to living kind and growing kindness. Caution: using this book causes happiness, connection, and a rich sense of community. Go buy this book!"

—ROB SCHEER, FOUNDER OF COMFORT CASES CHARITY FOR CHILDREN IN FOSTER CARE, DIGNITY AMBASSADOR, AND CNN HERO

"Kindness guru Leon Logothetis breaks ground with this innovative and unique part journal, part self-exploration exercise, and part life journey memoir.  **Go Be Kind** deeply immerses readers and encourages them to put in the work (the fun kind) that it takes to feel less alone. The secret? Kindness."

—LEFAIR MAGAZINE

"**Go Be Kind** is an actionable book that is also rich in imagination, creativity, and purpose. Use it to establish more meaningful connections in all aspects of life and inspire others to join in on the fun. Following the lessons and reading about Leon's worldwide kindness adventures will remind you that there's always time to be kind."

—LIGHT WATKINS, AUTHOR OF *BLISS MORE: HOW TO SUCCEED IN MEDITATION WITHOUT REALLY TRYING*

"Kindness is so clearly the heart medicine our world most needs! In **Go Be Kind**, Leon takes us on a great adventure in kindness ... with reminders about simple acts that can uplift our own spirit, and ripple out to help heal countless others."

—TARA BRACH, AUTHOR OF *RADICAL ACCEPTANCE*

"Real kindness takes practice and courage. This life changing journal is a profound and fun filled roadmap for developing deep compassion, empathy and self-awareness."

—BROOKS SINGER, MANAGER OF CUSTOMER EXPERIENCE AT SPIRITUAL GANGSTER

"**Go Be Kind** is a marvelous way for kids and parents to connect, simply by being kind **together**. A must-read!"

—DORO BUSH KOCH, FOUNDER OF BB&R WELLNESS CONSULTING AND AUTHOR OF *MY FATHER, MY PRESIDENT: A PERSONAL ACCOUNT OF THE LIFE OF GEORGE H. W. BUSH*

"There is magic inside these pages! This little journal will touch you and your family's life in a profoundly beautiful way."

—HEIDI GRANT, ASSOCIATE DIRECTOR OF THE MOTIVATION SCIENCE CENTER AT COLUMBIA UNIVERSITY AND BESTSELLING AUTHOR OF *NINE THINGS SUCCESSFUL PEOPLE DO DIFFERENTLY*

ALSO BY LEON LOGOTHETIS

Live, Love, Explore

The Kindness Diaries

Amazing Adventures of a Nobody

GO BE KIND

28½ Adventures
Guaranteed
to Make You Happier

A LIFE-CHANGING LITTLE JOURNAL

LEON LOGOTHETIS

BENBELLA

BenBella Books, Inc.
Dallas, TX

The first 25,000 postcards received will be guaranteed a book donation. All others may result in a donation at the author's discretion.

- -

BenBella

BenBella Books, Inc.
10440 N. Central Expressway, Suite 800
Dallas, TX 75231
www.benbellabooks.com | Send feedback to feedback@benbellabooks.com
BenBella is a federally registered trademark.

Printed in the United States of America
10 9 8 7 6 5 4

Library of Congress Cataloging-in-Publication Data is available upon request.
9781948836050 (trade cloth)
9781948836227 (e-book)

- -

Editing by Leah Wilson and Rachel Phares
Copyediting by Miki Alexandra Caputo
Proofreading by Sarah Vostok and Cape Cod Compositors, Inc.
Text design and composition by Kit Sweeney
Cover design by Sarah Avinger
Author photo by Andy Furneval
Printed by Lake Book Manufacturing

Distributed to the trade by Two Rivers Distribution, an Ingram brand
www.tworiversdistribution.com

Special discounts for bulk sales are available.
Please contact bulkorders@benbellabooks.com.

I created this journal for anyone
who has ever felt alone.

I see you.

This journal is your playground.
You can color, write all over it, rip
out the pages, explore your dreams.
Every page is another page from
your imagination. Let it run wild!

You're on your way!

☐ We'll check off
these boxes as we go.

But you get to start right now
just for opening this journal

   And beginning the greatest
   adventure of your life.

BEFORE WE BEGIN

OR WHAT
SOME PEOPLE CALL
THE INTRODUCTION

What you're holding in your hands isn't a book. It's not even a journal, really, though I'll call it that. It's something wilder, crazier, and—I'm just going to go out on a limb here— LIFE CHANGING.

Because kindness isn't something we read or write or think about.

It's something we **feel**.

Every day.

And when we feel **KINDNESS**, whether we're the ones giving it

or receiving it,

we get happy.

That's a fact.

And this not-book, kind-of journal, totally wild, crazy adventure is all about facts.

Like the fact that kindness is
the official language of love and
friendship and joy.

It is the unspoken energy that passes
between people

when we stop thinking about
ourselves for a minute

and start seeing—really **seeing**—each other.

Basically . . .

KINDNESS
MAKES
PEOPLE
FEEL
LESS
ALONE

(starting with yourself).

And we've all felt alone at some point. There are still days when I feel alone.

Although I have traveled the world on kindness, although I give lectures and speeches on kindness, although I try every day to #gobekind, I'm still human.

But I have also learned what it takes to be happy. So— you ready?

The big reveal . . .

4

The moment we've all been waiting for . . .

  The reason you picked up this journal . . .

If you want to be happy in life,

all

you

have

to

do

is

be

 KIND.

That's it.

Sometimes it feels like people have forgotten how to be kind. The world can be mean and loud and angry, and lately it seems like all we do is fight. But that is not who we are.

Because kindness lives in all of us, all the time.

It isn't something we have to find outside ourselves.

It's etched into our DNA—it's part of what makes us human.

And despite all the bad stuff in the world, kindness is what connects us to each other.

When you make someone feel less alone, **you** will feel less alone.

When you make someone feel better, **you** will feel better.

When you love, **you** will be loved.

We call it a

WIN-WIN.

It's an exact science. Honest. Endorphins and oxytocin and lots of other brain chemicals prove it. But I'm not a scientist (I once received 18% on a chemistry exam, so clearly I'm not).

What I am is a traveler. And what I've discovered on my travels is that there is no greater adventure on the planet than kindness. It beats climbing Mount Everest, or exploring the deep-sea wreckage of the Titanic, or hiking into the darkest recesses of the deepest caves.

> Because kindness will take you to the greatest mountaintops. It will lead you into incredible mysteries. It will show you the darkest parts of all of us . . . and then it will shine its magnificent light right into the very center of your being.

So why does this Englishman know so much about being kind? I mean, I look nothing like Mother Teresa.

The reason I know a few things about kindness is because I also know a few things about sadness.

See, years ago, I had everything I thought I ever wanted—a successful job, a fancy apartment, even a cool car. On the outside, I was the guy who had "made it."

Except I knew I wasn't that guy. I was the guy who was barely making it. I had all these things, but that didn't stop me from feeling profoundly alone.

And then I saw this little movie called **The Motorcycle Diaries**—the romanticized story of Che Guevara's early years traveling through South America.

It showed me a life filled with adventure and excitement, but most important, it showed me a life filled with connection. And I realized that was what I was missing—

CONNECTION.

So I decided to follow in Che's footsteps. I mean, I didn't become a famous revolutionary, but I found my own revolution. It was a revolution of kindness.

I walked from Times Square to the Hollywood sign on $5 a day, getting to know people all across America. And perhaps even more insane, I did the same thing across Europe—hitchhiking from Paris to Moscow—meeting people from all walks of life. I wanted to see what it meant to really connect to people on the street, to connect to the people I love, to connect back to myself.

I had seen how powerful that simple act of connecting could be, but I was usually the one receiving the kindness. I began to wonder, **What if I started to give it out?**

I had a theory: to be happy, I needed to go out and be kind. And I wanted to test it.

So I decided to do something REALLY crazy:

I didn't just hitchhike across America or Europe, I circumnavigated the WHOLE EARTH in a vintage yellow motorcycle with a sidecar and lots of attitude. I named the bike Kindness One—a little like Air Force One, but slightly yellower. This time, I didn't have $5 a day to get me through. Instead, I crossed the world relying entirely on the kindness of strangers and offering gifts of kindness in return. Sometimes those gifts were small. Sometimes they forever changed people's lives.

This journey of mine became a book, and later, a Netflix show called **The Kindness Diaries**, and then Netflix even asked me back for a second season (crazy!).

Through those adventures, I went out and met the world. I mean, not the whole world, because that would be ridiculous. But I met a lot of people in it—gay, straight, black, white, Bhutanese. I met Republicans and Democrats and people who collected ferrets. I was forced to connect with people. I was forced to connect with ferrets. And I had never been happier in my life. I also became a bit of an expert on human connection.

I went on to give speeches about the experience, and what I realized is that we are all capable of speaking that international language of connection . . .

KINDNESS.

We all want to reach out to others and make them feel less alone.

We all want to **be** less alone.

Like the Beatles, we just need a little help from our friends (and ourselves).

SO, WHAT IS THIS JOURNAL, LEON?

Funny you should ask . . .

First, I should tell you what this journal **isn't**. It isn't a book about random acts of kindness.

Because kindness isn't a random act.

It's an adventure.

GO BE KIND

is your treasure map.

And at the end of that road, you will find something better than gold.

You will find happiness.

That's a 100% money-back guarantee (just don't tell my publisher).

You will have the chance to change someone's life.

And when you change someone's life, you also change the **world**.

You just have to take a deep breath and dive into **KINDNESS**.

The Ground Rules

GO BE KIND offers 28½ adventures in kindness.

You can do one a day.

But you don't have to.

(You can do one every two days, you could do two a day, you can do them however you want.)

You can do them alone

or with friends

or with your ferret.

If you're a parent, you can do them with your child.

If you're a kid, you can do them with your mum or dad or grandparents (or everyone!).

You can be 10 years old or 110 years old.

It doesn't matter where you're from or what you believe in or who you are.

KINDNESS
+ YOU

HAPPINESS

You can take your time.

Or you can speed through because you need to connect, and you don't have time to wait.

You can do all of them.

Or you can skip some
(though I highly suggest you don't).

GO BE KIND
isn't called Go Be Perfect.

Because that's impossible. No one does kindness perfectly. I certainly don't. Just ask anyone who knows me.

>This isn't about being kind every moment of every day. You can still have bad days. I mean, sometimes you might even be mean (highly unsuggested).

The adventures in this book will show you that kindness isn't about never having a bad day—it's about having a good life.

Some of the adventures will be easy,
  some will be hard,
    some will be scary,

but they will all be fun.

Some will ask you to use your phone. Some will have you turn it off.

Some will require a postage stamp. Some will require you to dance.

Some will suggest you have scissors, tape, or glue. Almost all will require a pen.

And then there's the one where you talk to a tree (no, really, you must talk to a tree).

Some adventures will tempt you to adopt a dog.

Some will tempt you to change the world.

Spoiler alert: **you will change the world.**

And yes, there might be times you are tempted to quit (because you're human).

But it's like anything in life . . .

The more you give, the more you get.

And I promise, by giving kindness, by doing every adventure, by trusting this crazy English chap who has

CIRCUMNAVIGATED THE GLOBE

on kindness, you'll find that you'll get so much more than you ever expected to receive.

You will get
(list of other guaranteed side effects):

Happiness
Peace of Mind
Excitement
Super Funny Stuff
Faith
Friendship
Dreams
Compassion
Strength
Connection

Because the opposite of kindness isn't cruelty—it's being alone.

And when we're kind to others, we make them feel less alone. We show them that **I see you**. We show them that they matter.

Because kindness isn't about being walked on or pushed over. Kindness is about finding the strength to see how amazing other people are (and how amazing we are). Kindness gives us the strength to be brave. It gives us the faith to believe in ourselves.

Did you ever watch **Mister Rogers' Neighborhood**? We didn't have him in England when I was growing up, but when I came to the US I realized what us British kids had been missing out on. Mister Rogers taught an entire generation that in order to be happy all they had to do was go be kind. Months before Fred Rogers passed away, he wrote a letter to his fans. He told them,

"I would like to tell you what I often told you when you were much younger. I like you just the way you are. It's such a good feeling to know that we're lifelong friends."

So are you ready to be **friends**?

To tell you the truth, we became friends the minute you picked up this journal.

So let's do this! Hop into my motorcycle sidecar—we're about to be adventure buddies. I've been here before, so I kind of know the road.

Let's go be happy.

All we have to do is

GO BE KIND.

ADVENTURE #1

WHAT DOES
KINDNESS MEAN
TO YOU?

Look up from this book right now.

What do you see?

Do you see a blue sky?

  Do you see a couple holding hands?

    Do you see your TV?

Do you see an opportunity to be kind?

Because I do.

  No matter where you are,
  no matter what the world looks like,

  there is always an opportunity to

Be Kind.

But what does that mean?

> **I DON'T KNOW, LEON. YOU'RE THE "EXPERT."**

Kindness means something to everyone.

To me, it means

MAKING SOMEONE FEEL LESS ALONE.

It means

STOPPING TO SEE SOMEONE.

Like really see them—

see everything that makes them
who they are,

the hidden and magical space inside us all.

I gave you space to tell me (and your other new best friend, this journal) . . .

Looky here

Don't feel like writing anything?
That's OK. No problem.

I gave you space to draw something
instead.

Don't feel like drawing anything?
That's cool too.

You want to **SING A SONG?**
DO A DANCE?

WRITE A POEM?

Because **KINDNESS** is really just
an expression of who we are—
who we are at the very center of our hearts.

The place few people ever get to see.
And even fewer people get to know.

But it's when you stop and really see someone,

that they get to see you too.

Now take your definition,
      your drawing,
        your song,
          your poem,
or just the simple line "Kindness means

_____ to me"

and share it with someone.

How **embarrassing!**

Yes.

In order to **GO BE KIND,**
we have to share where kindness lives in us.

You can tell a friend, you can tell your mum, you can tell Facebook.

I dare you.

   I **double** dare you.

Wanna hear a secret?

You've just done the first adventure.

But there are so *so* so *so* SO *so* so **SO** many more.

We're just getting started.

Live your kindness out loud
 just for today
   and then watch it

EXPLODE

in your heart.

You did it! Time to check off your box
and say hooray:

☐ The path to happiness
is laid with bricks of kindness.
I just laid the first brick! Yippee!

ADVENTURE #2

WHO IS THE
KINDEST PERSON
YOU KNOW?

A little story about me.

I was a pretty **LONELY** kid.

(I mean, I've been a lonely adult too, but we'll get to that.)

Growing up, I was super-duper when-is-this-going-to-end lonely. I was bullied and teased and ate most lunches by myself. I didn't like school. I didn't have friends. I was even made fun of by teachers. **Teachers.** Nothing will ruin fifth grade like being teased by a 40-year-old paid to be your friend. It was not a good time in the life of Leon Logothetis.

At times I felt broken. So broken that I didn't know if I could ever be fixed.

But then, one day, I started an after-school program with a new teacher, Mrs. Mann. Mrs. Mann saw something in me that no one else did.

She told me . . .

And over time, I did.

I started to see that I wasn't bad or a loser. I started liking school.

OK, fine, maybe **like** is pushing it. But I didn't hate going there.

Mrs. Mann did something so absolutely revolutionary that she changed my life forever.

SHE WAS KIND.

We all have a Mrs. Mann.

That one person who saw something in us that we couldn't see in ourselves.

The person who LIFTED us up,

who made us believe we were special.

Maybe it's your mum or dad or teacher or boss or friend or pastor or a stranger on the street.

Maybe it's someone you spoke to five minutes ago.

Maybe it's someone you haven't talked to in 50 years.

And if you don't have someone like this in your life, then you can call **me** your Mrs. Mann.

Because I'll tell you right now the same thing Mrs. Mann told me:

I believe in you.
I know you have so much inside to share.
I hope you can start to see that too.

But if you **do** have a Mrs. Mann in your life,

it's time to let them know.

Welcome to **Adventure #2**.

It's not all about writing or drawing or sharing things on Facebook/Snapchat/ Instagram/Twitter.

It's about

CONNECTING.

With the people you know.

The ones who have reminded you what kindness can do.

The ones who helped to change your life.

Call them.

Find them if you haven't talked to them in a while.

(Behold the power of social media!)

Reach out to them and say

THANK YOU:

Because Mrs. Mann saved my life. And there's a good chance someone saved yours.

Let them know what they did.

And if you can't find them, or they're no longer with us? Send them a message.

Yes, a message.

You can probably record your voice on your phone. If so, record a message for that person.

Tell them everything you would say if you were talking on the phone.

Remind yourself of what they did for you.

HONOR THEM. HONOR YOU.

They're listening.

I promise.

You did it!

☐ Today I honored the person who believed in me, and I reminded myself that I am worth believing in.

ADVENTURE #3

KINDNESS
COMPLIMENTS

You know when you're just walking down the street and then a complete stranger stops you and says, "You know what, you look really happy right now, and you just made my day!"

What? That hasn't happened to you?

Well, **TIME TO CHANGE THAT.**

Because you're about to start a wave of kindness.

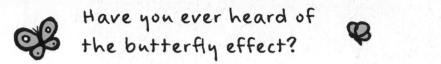

Have you ever heard of the butterfly effect?

When a single butterfly flaps their wings on one side of the world

they can cause a storm on the other.

You can be that butterfly.

Right now.

Today.

on to **Adventure #3**.

Day 3 and you're already changing the world????

I told you that might happen.

Because in order to change the world

   all you have to do is change one life.

Yup.

Just one.

And the most beautiful way to change one life?

So let's do it. Today, you're hitting the streets or the office park or the mall or your school or the grocery store or wherever else you can go where you are going to see PEOPLE

and then you're going to compliment them.

OH, THAT'S EASY, LEON.

"NICE SHOES," AND THEN WALK AWAY.

Stop. Right. There.

This isn't about complimenting what people are wearing.

It's about complimenting **who they are**.

And because kindness isn't always easy, we're throwing in an extra-special, supercalifragilistic twist.

We're gonna make this a scavenger hunt.

You're going to need to find someone

Who looks lonely

Who doesn't
look like you

Who looks
sad or angry

Who just did
something nice for
someone else

and you aren't going to compliment
their shoes.

Oh, no.

You're going to make their day!!!!

Excited yet? You should be. Maybe you could say . . .

"I love your laugh!"

"You just put a smile on my face."

"That was really nice what you just did."

OR IF NOTHING ELSE . . .

"I love your shoes!"

BUT THEY HAVE TO BE REALLY GOOD SHOES.

AND THEN LET THEM KNOW . . .

"You just made my day!"

THE SMALLEST GESTURE OF KINDNESS CAN HAVE A MASSIVE IMPACT.

Because once you start flapping your wings

and **they** start flapping **their** wings,

that connection can be felt across
the globe.

Because if one butterfly can make a storm,

a group of butterflies can start
a revolution.

We remind the world that kindness is
more than an act.

It is the language of how we connect.

And by the time you've finished
Adventure #3, you will have just

CHANGED THE WORLD.

I wasn't lying.

You did it!

By changing one
life, we change the world,
and today, I changed
the world. I mean, that's
some crazy stuff, but I
felt it happening.

ADVENTURE #4

OXYGEN MASK

Sometimes the one person we forget to be kind to is ourselves.

Every day we tell ourselves lies
    without even realizing they're lies.
We say . . .

I need to lose weight
I'm never going to meet anyone to love
I'm not pretty enough
I'm not funny enough
I'm not cool enough
I don't have enough followers
I don't have enough money
I don't have enough friends
I don't have an English accent (kidding, kidding!)
I don't have enough
I am not enough . . .

But you have everything you need.

You are so absolutely perfect that when your parents met and made a child . . .
they made **YOU**.

I mean, how crazy is that? Out of all the possibilities in the world, **you** were the miracle.

And you were brought here to share that miracle.

To love yourself.

To love other people.

To know what it means to be loved.

You know how on the airplane they tell you to put the oxygen mask on yourself first?

That's because we can't save anyone else until we can save ourselves.

But first we have to believe we're worth saving.

We have to see all the ways in which we are so absolutely perfect that we were chosen to be born.

But enough from me.

I want to hear it from YOU.

Imagine I'm your flight attendant, standing at the front of the plane. I'm showing you how to put on the oxygen mask. Except this time it is not a drill.

"You need to put on your oxygen mask right now!" I scream in a way that makes people laugh nervously.

Instead of an actual oxygen mask (because that would be weird), I want you to get a pen

and write about how awesome you are.

You can't use the words

NOT
ALMOST MAYBE
COULD BE

Take the best parts of yourself

and go **BIG** with them.

Write a love song like you're John Legend.

Write a sonnet like you're Shakespeare.

Write a haiku like you're Kobayashi Issa (that's a really famous Haiku poet).

Just write about all the things that make you you.

Do it right here.

Do it right now.

Don't turn the page, don't pass Go, don't collect $200

until you've reminded yourself why the universe chose YOU to come to earth.

I'm going to be coming through the cabin and making sure you did it.

Don't worry.

No one will ever see it (except your super secret's-safe-with-me journal).

In fact, don't share it with anyone.

This one is just for you.

I never knew how awesome I was until I stopped telling myself that I wasn't. I'm actually a bit of a legend (like John Legend). When I see how kindness can change the world, I realize that I can change the world too.

ADVENTURE #5

WHAT STOPS YOU FROM BEING KIND?

I'm not saying you're **mean**. For starters, you're reading a book on kindness. (I'm pretty sure a mean person would never do that.)

But the truth is all of us can be kinder.

Every day.

And that includes me.

> Because kindness is about more than manners.

> It's about **seeing everyone else** around us.

Have you ever read the book **The Little Prince**? It's about a little English boy who travels the whole world to find friends because on his planet, he is totally, utterly alone.

Just kidding. He's not English.

But he is a boy searching the whole universe for kindness. Until finally, he lands on a planet filled with beautiful flowers, and one lonely fox.

A very important fox.

After the prince and the fox become friends, the prince must leave to go and meet more people. The fox is sad to see his new friend leave and promises that if the prince will spend just a little bit more time with him, he will tell him a secret, a very important secret.

You want to hear it?

"It is only with the heart that one can see rightly; what is essential is invisible to the eye."

Pretty smart fox.

Because we cannot see kindness. But when we see other people, we can feel kindness in our hearts.

Usually, though, we're too . . .

BUSY SHY
SCARED TIRED
STRESSED

to reach out to someone else.
Today's adventure is an easy one.

A POP QUIZ actually.

Now, before you turn the page,
get out your pen.

It's OK, I'll wait.

Don't jump ahead.

Got it? Great.
When you see the following
quiz, don't think. Just answer.

Ready?

If this takes you more than
thirty seconds, you took too long.

What stops you from being kind?

- ☐ I'm terrified I'm going to get hurt if I share my heart with the world.
- ☐ I'm angry that the world is so hard and mean at times!
- ☐ I'm shy and I don't really know what to say.
- ☐ I'm not shy and I **still** don't know what to say.
- ☐ I don't want to get embarrassed, or worse, rejected.
- ☐ I feel like I live on a lonely planet.
- ☐ I feel like a lonely fox.
- ☐ Other: _____

Don't move.

Don't turn the page.

Don't check your phone

or put something in your cart
on Amazon.

Don't do any of the things we use to
avoid being uncomfortable.

Kindness is about being comfortable
with the uncomfortable.

Sit with your answer for a moment. Even
if it hurts a little.

Because whatever is stopping you from
connecting with others

is the same thing that stops you from
being really, truly happy.

We all have that dark place, that big hurt, the thing that gets in the way

every time we want to reach out to someone else.

Every time we want to be honest with ourselves.

What is it?

I'll tell you mine:

I felt **Alone** for a lot of my life.

See, you can do it.
Your turn.

Now that you've written it down . . .

Sit with it.

Comfort it.

HOLD ITS HAND.

And begin to figure out a way
to work together.

You're not going to fix it in one day.

Change takes TIME.

I decided to heal my big hurt by
connecting with other people.

That doesn't mean that I am never alone.

But my big hurt of aloneness has been
healed—I moved from hurt to happy.

And no, that didn't happen overnight.

But it can start
RIGHT NOW for you.

Feel free to rip your
BIG HURT out of
this journal and put it
somewhere where you can
look at it.

How can you start to heal
your big hurt today

so that you can be happy?

You did it!

We all have a big hurt that stands between us and the world. Today, I started to heal my hurt so I could share my heart.

ADVENTURE #6

LEARN FROM
THE BEST

Time to hit the ~~mean~~ kind streets.

There's a story about a little girl whose mother just had a baby. When the parents bring the baby home, the little girl asks to speak to the baby alone.

The parents let her but watch from the doorway.

The little girl leans in to the baby and says,

"Tell me what God looks like. I have started to forget."

God can mean anything.

God can mean

LOVE   LIGHT   HOPE

HONESTY   MAGIC

MIRACLES

And children are connected to all those things.

Children remember the face of God.

That's why they make the best teachers.

And it's why we need to learn from them.

Last year, I was giving a speech at a middle school, and after my speech, a little girl came up to me. She looked really shy. I was getting ready to start telling her more about loneliness and kindness when she interrupted me.

MR. LEON, KINDNESS ISN'T ROCKET SCIENCE, YOU KNOW.

Leave it to a kid to take your life's work and sum it up in one sentence.

Because she was right. Kindness isn't rocket science. Anyone can do it.

All we have to do is get out there.

So grab your journal and your pen and **GO FIND A KID**.

That's easier for some than others.

It's really easy if you **are** a kid, or a parent and kid doing this together!

You might have a child in the next room.

Or you might need to stop a parent and ask them if you can ask their child a question about kindness.

Show them this journal.

Explain what you're doing.

Nine times out of ten, people will say yes to kindness.

Trust me. I have traveled the globe asking strangers for help.

If they know why you're doing it,

they will want to go on the adventure too.

Use this book as your notebook, like you're an old-school journalist.

Working the beat.

Getting the lead.

Asking a kid.

And if you **are** a kid (awesome—you are a kindness leader!), ask a friend.

Then get ready to ask yourself the same question.

But don't answer with your right hand (or left hand, if that's your dominant one).

They say when we write with our nondominant hands
     we get in touch with our inner child.
          We remember the face of God.

So, with your opposite hand, answer that same question:

WHAT DOES KINDNESS MEAN TO YOU?

_____

_____

_____

_____

_____

_____

_____

_____

_____

_____

_____

_____

_____

_____

Close your eyes.

Think about your answer.

Remember when you were a child
(or if you **are** a kid, then you get to cheat!):

how much
it meant to
be kind

to
be loved

to be connected

to realize that the face of God
is the face of kindness.

We can all remember what
kindness looks like if we ask.

You did it!

☐ I got to see kindness through the eyes of a child. And I got to see the kid in me!

REALLY QUICK, SUPER IMPORTANT, INCREDIBLY MOTIVATIONAL STORY ABOUT KINDNESS

"In all the years that have passed, there has never been another child like you. You have the capacity for anything."

—Pablo Casals, musician and composer

Time for a little kindness huddle. You know, like in football, the American kind.

We're going to put our heads together.

Take a few deep breaths. And let's go over the game plan.

Have you completed every adventure so far?

If you haven't, that's OK.

I'm not judging.

(How unkind would that be?)

The worst thing if you haven't is that nothing has happened. Not a lot to lose there.

But imagine what you have to gain!

As you might remember, a few years ago, I filmed a little show called **The Kindness Diaries**. That was my slightly brilliant, absolutely insane idea to circumnavigate the globe on a vintage motorcycle (with a sidecar built just for friends like you).

When we finished taping the show, we were so proud of what we had done. I mean, we had shown the best of humanity—people being kind to each other, people connecting from all over the world. It was a story of hope and love and adventure, and I figured everyone would want to buy it.

Guess what? No one did.

There is a special kind of heartbreak when you pour EVERYTHING YOU ARE into an idea, and then no one else seems to believe in it. And I began to believe that I had been wrong all along.

Maybe the world had become too jaded for kindness.

Maybe the world didn't want to connect.

There were so many days during this time when I wanted to give up. When I felt absolutely defeated and heartbroken and like the biggest loser on the planet. But I knew that kindness deserved more than that. It deserved to be fought for.

So I kept fighting. And I realized that as long as I didn't give up, I didn't feel so defeated or heartbroken or like the BIGGEST loser on the planet. As long as I believed, there was a chance that someone else might believe too.

And they did.

This little company called Netflix saw it, and they thought that kindness was exactly what the world needed. In fact, they liked it so much they asked me to do another season, so I traveled from Alaska to Argentina in a 50-year-old yellow Beetle. (My motorcycle asked to be retired—he's old, OK!)

Humans are a pretty incredible bunch. We're stubborn as donkeys, but we soar like eagles.

And you, my friend, also have the capacity for anything.

And that includes these

adventures.

I know you can do it. And I know just how much you have to gain. (I promise, it's a lot.)

So, take a second. Think about the adventures you just completed, and then without even really thinking, just feeling it with your heart, tell me on a scale of 1-10 . . .

HOW HAPPY ARE YOU?

Write it down on the happiness scale.

It's OK if you're only a 1. That's what I'm here for.

And we have so much more fun ahead of us!

ADVENTURE #7

FIND A
KINDNESS BUDDY

You can't be kind alone.
I mean, you **can**.
To yourself.

But then you need to get out there.

    You need to be kind to others.

        You need to strengthen your
        kindness muscle.

But just like with any exercise, we are more likely to go to the gym when we have a buddy than when we are alone.

So, it's time to ask someone to be your Kindness Buddy.

They'll be there for

SUPPORT
IDEAS
CHEERLEADING
FRIENDSHIP
TO LAUGH AT THIS SILLY ENGLISHMAN, LEON

But most important, they'll be there to join you in being kind.

They can do the journal with you

and then you get to be their Kindness Buddy too!

Or they can watch from a close distance.

They can be

- Your friend
- Your partner
- Your teacher
- Your coworker
- Your child
- Your parent
- Your dog

Yes, even your dog.

As long as it is someone who is willing to listen to you, and to love you at the end of the day.

(See, dogs apply—and cats too!)

But a human is probably preferred.
Because, you know, they talk.

Think of someone who could use this
journal too.
Maybe someone going through a tough
time in life.

Maybe they lost their job, maybe they
just had their heart broken, maybe a
big plan didn't work out, maybe they're
depressed or anxious or
lonely, or maybe they
just need someone to
reach out and say . . .

Will you be
my Kindness
Buddy?

The Kindness Buddy Contract is simple.

You will call your buddy every few days to check in.

You will report on your kindness adventures.

You will let them know if you have quit or want to quit the adventures.

And if you don't call, they will call you. If neither of you calls, I will call you both! Joke. Kind of.

Got your person?

Great! Give them a call, send them a text, DM them.

. . .

. . .

. . .

. . .

. . .

. . .

They say yes?
Awesome!

☐ Now you can sign your kindness pledge. Ready?

KINDNESS PLEDGE

I, _____, hereby assign
_____ to be my Kindness
Buddy. As part of this contract, I will
check in with them every few days. I will
report on my kindness adventures. I will
let them know if I have quit or want to
quit the journal. And if I don't connect
with them, they have agreed to contact
me. They will see how I'm doing. They will
check in on my adventures. And if
needed, they will kick me in
the butt.

In Kindness,

_____
Your Signature Here

WINNIE APPROVED

ADVENTURE #8

SUPER AGENT 007
SECRET MISSION
IMPOSSIBLE THING
THAT YOU CAN
TOTALLY DO

So, whatever you do, don't turn the page yet.

I know that's not easy.

I know that as I said that, you probably just turned the page.

But I promise you

the secret mission will be so much more fun

if we keep it a secret for just a few more pages.

That's right. You're going on a

SUPER AGENT 007 SECRET MISSION IMPOSSIBLE THING THAT YOU CAN TOTALLY DO.

A few of them, really.

But this is the first.

We're going back out there in the world.

You know . . . to the kind streets

or school hallways

or the mall

or the office park.

Or anywhere you go where there are lots of people you've never met before.

x x x x x x x x x x x x x x x x x x x x x x x x x x x x x x x x x x x

When I travel the world, I always go to the most popular part of town, like Times Square or the Eiffel Tower, because people are happiest when they are around other people. They're more likely to take a chance on kindness, to connect with an absolute stranger. Even a bald English guy on a yellow motorcycle asking to sleep on their couch. And if I can ask random people if I

can sleep on their couch in Times Square,
I promise you can complete your . . .

And I don't want you to turn the page
until you get there.

It's OK, I'll wait. Head anywhere there
are lots of people you've never met
before—or if you're at work or school,
find some people you don't know.

You there yet?

Great!

Now, look around.

I want you to find three people who don't
look like you.

If you're a woman, they're a man.

If you're black, they're Asian.

If you're from Oklahoma, they look like they're from somewhere else.

If you're from somewhere else, they look like they're from Oklahoma.

When we stop and give each other a chance, we give happiness a chance too.

You're not asking them to sign anything or do anything (like let you sleep on their couch—we'll save that for the sequel).

You're just asking them to connect.

OK, ready?

TURN THE PAGE.

SUPER AGENT 007
SECRET MISSION IMPOSSIBLE
THING THAT YOU CAN
TOTALLY DO

Ask each person you find today if they have two minutes to answer some questions about kindness.

Tell them you're doing this crazy journal (written by an even crazier guy)

called  GO BE KIND

and part of the book is that you have to do adventures in kindness.

Here's how your conversation might go . . .

YOU: Will you do a kindness adventure with me?
THEM: Sure. Sounds great! I love talking to strangers about kindness.
AWESOME. My first question is, When was the last time you felt alone?
THEY ANSWER.
When was the last time you felt loved?
THEY ANSWER.
What would you do if you won the lottery?
THEY ANSWER.
OK, last question. What does kindness mean to you?

Don't write any of it down. You're not here to take notes.

You're here to LISTEN.
You're here to CONNECT.

Then, when they're done, ask if they want to hear your answers.

Tell them when you last felt lonely, when you last felt loved. Tell them what you would do if you won the lottery. And then tell them what kindness means to you.

See how similar your responses were. Because despite our differences, we have all felt alone, and we have all felt loved (and if you haven't, message me right now on Facebook and I will tell you how truly amazing you are).

www.facebook.com/TheKindnessGuy

It is absolutely mind-blowing how connecting with a stranger changes our whole day. How it makes us believe in each other again. How it makes us happy.

When we connect with someone else's feelings, when we realize that we have felt how they feel, or we feel how they have felt, we create this crazy, amazing, magical thing between two people. It's called **empathy.**

Here's the secret of the mission:

EMPATHY

EQUALS

KINDNESS

EQUALS

HAPPINESS

You did it!

☐ Today I talked to someone I had never met before, and I found out the fastest route to happiness is to connect with someone's heart. Because when I do, I connect with my heart too!

ADVENTURE #9

TURN YOUR BACK
ON THE WORLD AND
THE WORLD TURNS
ITS BACK ON YOU,
CARE FOR THE WORLD
AND THE WORLD
WILL CARE FOR YOU

Through my adventures, I have met a lot of people who have been forgotten by the world. They live in either poverty or illness or just plain aloneness. They wake up every day and feel like the world has turned its back on them. And there is nothing more heartbreaking than feeling like someone has turned their back on you.

It's pretty much the reason for everything bad in the world:

WAR
VIOLENCE
GREED
ANGER

They aren't caused by evil.
They're caused by

ISOLATION
LONELINESS
FEAR
PAIN

But often we forget what it means to be alone (even though we have all been alone).

Because sometimes life GETS BUSY.

Sometimes life GETS GOOD.

And we forget that others are HURTING.

Today we are all going to be reminded of what it's like when the world turns its back.

We're going to feel what it's like when we turn our backs on the world.

And then we're going to fix it.

We're going to look each other straight in the eye and say, "I CARE ABOUT YOU."

It's time to find a friend.

Or a group of friends.

I mean, you can do this adventure with a stranger if you like.

You'll get extra special brownie points.

But if you're not in it for brownie
points, then just ask a friend at
work, at school, at home. Or ask your
Kindness Buddy.

Set your phone's timer for one minute.

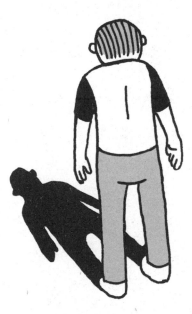

And then ask your
friend to turn their
back on you.

Don't say
anything.

Ignore each other
completely.

When I give my speeches, I ask people in the auditorium to do this. When that first minute is up you can hear a pin drop.

Because everyone can feel the loneliness.

And loneliness is silent.

It empties us. It takes the music away.

o o o o o o o o o o o o o o o o o o o o o o o o o o o o o

Don't try to fill that silence with laughter. Let your heart feel it.

Let that minute last.

And then, when it's up, see what it's like to turn your back. Have your friend or total stranger (brownie points!) turn around, and then you turn the other way.

Stand there for a minute. Feel how much it hurts when we hurt someone else.

Feel the isolation. And the loneliness. And the fear.

Feel the pain of turning **your** back.

Can you feel the loneliness of making someone else feel alone?

Can you feel how it hurts to hurt someone else?

Go ahead and share about it here. Draw it.

Let the tears come to your eyes.

Feel the loneliness of the world
when we turn our backs.

Feel the loneliness of your own heart
when the world turns its back.

And then (like I promised)

WE FIX IT.

We turn to face each other. We look each other in the eyes. We say, "I care about you."

And we realize that sometimes that's all we really need to do to fix the world.

And then **remember that feeling** every time you see someone who is alone. When someone is angry or greedy or violent. They aren't evil. They are just standing in the shadow of the world's back. And that can be a cold and lonely place . . . until kindness shows up. Until we turn around and say, "I am here for you, friend. I am here right now."

☐ When I turn my back on the world, I can no longer feel. When the world turns its back on me, I feel alone. When I turn around and say "I care about you," I realize the world cares about me too. I fix the world a little bit. And I get to fix me too!

ADVENTURE #10

CELL PHONE
ROULETTE

OK, this is a big one.

It might feel **WEIRD**

or SCARY

or downright SILLY.

Which means it might just be one of the most important adventures in this journal.

Because anything that feels weird or scary or downright silly is bound to make you HAPPY.

- -

I remember the first day I set off to cross the world on that yellow motorcycle, Kindness One. I just needed one person to help me, to give me my first tank of gas, in order to, you know, start circumnavigating the earth. Except no one would say yes. I was only 30 minutes into my journey, and I wanted to quit.

But I knew that happiness requires work—and so does kindness.

So I kept going. And then I found a brave man who bought me my first tank of gas, and jump-started my dream.

//

Now it's your turn to do something weird, scary, or downright silly.

Happiness demands bravery—and now is your chance to be brave.

READY?

Great! Because it's time to play cell phone roulette.

Go ahead and grab your phone.

Right now.

No, not later.
Now.

Go to your
contacts.

And then get
ready and scroll through.

Just like a roulette table. Or the showcase
showdown wheel from **The Price Is Right**.

Put your hand on the first name and then

SPIIIIIIIIIINNNNNN!!!

Did it stop?

Awesome.

Who did it stop on?

☐ A FRIEND?

 A FORMER FRIEND?

 SOMEONE YOU PROMISED
YOU WOULD CALL AND
NEVER DID?

☐ A SCHOOLMATE?

☐ YOUR SPOUSE?

WELL, GUUUESSSS
WHAAAAAAAT?

You get to call or text them.

That's right.

You get to connect with them.

Right now.

HIT THAT NAME.
LET IT RING.
TEXT THEM A MESSAGE.

Tell them you saw their name in your phone and wanted to see how they were.

> You can tell them about the journal if you want.
>
> > Or you can just let them know that you wanted to reach out.

Ask them how they are.

See what's been going on in their life.

If it's someone you talk to all the time, tell them what they mean to you.

And if it's someone who is hard to call (maybe someone who has hurt you or whom you hurt),

> say whatever you need to say to make that call or text easier.

> Whatever you need to say to set yourself free.

We can restart old friendships or begin new ones.

And who knows what the call or text might mean to that person.

> It might just be the exact message they need at that exact moment.

Happiness comes when we embrace feeling weird or scary or downright silly.

When we **GO BE BRAVE**.

You did it!

I got brave, played the game, and put a smile on someone's face—and my smile got a little bit bigger too!

ADVENTURE #11

STARTING AT ZERO

Guess what?!

You're not perfect. No one is!

Even Gandhi wasn't perfect. I swear.
I knew the man personally (that's a lie).

But I know this: We are all
HUMAN.

And humans are flawed and beautiful
and complicated and lovely and
definitely, no matter what,
super-duper imperfect.

But that's OK. We don't grow without
making mistakes. And sometimes we
learn the most from our biggest ones.

First, though, we have to realize we
made them.

Now it's time to remember a moment
when you weren't perfect.

And we've all had those moments.

I might have become an accidental expert in kindness, but that doesn't mean I haven't been mean.

When I was a kid, I was bullied every day at school. So when I got home, I did the same thing to my little brother. I bullied him.

People call it kicking the dog (or cat, or ferret, if you will).

At school, I was the lowest person on the totem pole, but when I got home, my little brother was even lower. And so I took out all my pain and anger and frustration on him.

I bullied him for years. One day, we were walking to a nearby park when I saw a bush of stinging nettles. If you don't know what those are, they're like really mean plants, and their name is dead on. They sting. A lot.

I pushed him into those stinging nettles. Yup, Mr. Kindness Expert shoved his brother into a burning bush. There goes my career!

I remember my brother crying afterward, covered in red welts. He asked me, "Why did you do that, Leon?"

And at the time, I didn't really know.

It took me a lot of years to realize that sometimes hurt people don't know what else to do besides hurt other people.

So now it's your turn to remember one time when you were really mean.

It could have been when you bullied someone when you were a kid

or when you bullied someone yesterday.

It could be when you recently gossiped about a friend, or maybe did something worse.

Have you ever betrayed someone?

Have you ever broken someone's heart?

It's OK. We all have.

I have been mean.

I have betrayed people.

I have broken people's hearts.

So think back.

What is the one moment where you most acted like a total zero?

It doesn't matter if you've never told anyone before.

It's even better if you've never told anyone before.

Your secret is safe with me (and your other BFF, this journal).

What is the one thing you have done that you haven't forgiven yourself for?

Go ahead and write it here.

OK.

Now, here's the hard part.

Are you ready?

Because kindness demands that we **believe** that we are kind.

We can't connect with other people if we are holding on to our own

GUILT
SHAME
FEAR

around something we have done.

When we let go of our old baggage, our hands become free to reach out to others.

So it's time to let it go (like in the movie **Frozen**—good luck getting that song out of your head!).

Yes, that's right.

Here comes

THE HARD PART.

It's time to understand your own worst moment.

Why did you do what you did?

Were you kicking the dog? Taking your frustrations out on someone with even less than you?

What was the reason lurking underneath?

Were you

EMBARRASSED?

SCARED?

LONELY?

HURT?

ANGRY?

DEPRESSED?

Did you even mean to do it?

Did you feel bad as soon as you did it?

Did you even realize you had done something wrong?

Because there are only a few evil people in the world. And they aren't buying books about kindness.

You aren't evil.
You aren't bad.
You aren't a zero.

You are just an imperfect human being, which means you **are** a human being.

Welcome to the club.

But there is a way out. And that out is in understanding the **why**.

So ask yourself, Why did you do it?

WRITE YOUR ANSWER HERE.

Sometimes knowing the answer is all we need to set ourselves free.

You did it!

I'm just a human being. I've made some mistakes. But realizing why I made them makes me feel way more free!

ADVENTURE #12

ENDING AT HERO

Being a  isn't that hard.

It just means that you're willing to **GO BE KIND**.

That's literally all it takes to be a hero.

To.

So let's do it.
Let's be heroes.

There are people in this world who are
considered heroes for doing huge and
amazing things. And then there are
some heroes who have changed the world
simply by being kind.

Have you ever heard of
Evan Fernandez?

Evan Fernandez is a Spanish runner.
In 2011 he was competing against
Kenyan racer Abel Mutai. Abel was
in the lead, but 30 feet out from
the finish line, he slowed down. Evan
realized that Abel thought he had
already crossed the finish line. He
thought he had won the race.

Evan could have breezed right past
Abel and accepted first place. But
he didn't.

He chose to be kind. He showed Abel
where the finish line was. He allowed his
competitor to run ahead and win the race.

Evan could have won first place that day.

But he did something else.

He became a **HERO** instead.

We can all slow down and help someone else. We can all be a hero to someone.

And we don't even need a cape (or running shoes) to do it. Because kindness isn't a costume.

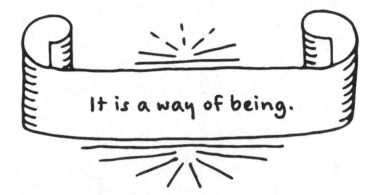

It is a way of being.

And the best way to be a hero is to make someone else feel less alone.

Today (if possible) you're going to be a hero to the person you hurt.

Ready to get out your pen?
Great. I thought so.

On the next pages, you're going to write the name of the person you hurt. And then you are going to put their contact information down—phone number, email, mailing address.

However you can connect with them.

Next, you're going to write down what you did, just as you did earlier, but this time, you're going to add **why** you did it. Remember how it set you free? Well, it might just set that other person free too.

We've all been hurt before.

But we don't always think about what caused the other person to do it.

We think about what **we** might have done **wrong**. What we might have done DIFFERENTLY.

We forget that most people aren't mean because they are evil.

They are mean because they are hurt. They are mean because they are suffering.

      They

          May

               Even

                    Be

                         Broken.

Years ago, I asked my brother out to lunch. I told him I was sorry for bullying him when we were kids. I told him that I was so beaten down at school, I just wanted someone to beat up who was weaker than me. I was a hurt kid. And I took it all out on him.

It wasn't an easy conversation, but through it we began to **HEAL**.

Now is your chance to explain the real reason you acted as you did.

Share that you were

- SCARED
- ANGRY
- EMBARRASSED
- HURT
- LONELY
- DEPRESSED

142

Now go back to your card and at the bottom write, "I'm sorry. I know I made a mistake and I want to make it right."

Finished? Great. I'm sure you know what's next.

It's time to make that call.

Write that email.

Send that letter.

If they respond, say what you have to say and then listen to what they have to say.

In order to be a hero, you have to be a hear-o.

When we listen, truly listen to someone, we can, if only for a moment, put ourselves in their shoes.

And feel how we hurt that person.

Talk about EMPATHY.

BUT LEON, WHAT IF I CAN'T FIND THE PERSON I HURT?

That's OK too. You can still fill out your card. You can still write the email or the letter. You can send it to yourself. You can send it to your Kindness Buddy.

In fact, definitely send it to your Kindness Buddy.

And find another way to **GO BE KIND**.

- **VOLUNTEER.**
- **STAND UP FOR SOMEONE ELSE.**
- **STOP AND LISTEN TO SOMEONE IN PAIN.**

You will be embarking on the great act of kindness.

And kindness is the only cape a real hero needs.

I got to be a hero today just by being kind. Next time, I'll wear a cape.

REALLY QUICK, SUPER IMPORTANT, AND INCREDIBLY MOTIVATIONAL STORY ABOUT KINDNESS

"You're off to Great Places! Today is your day! Your mountain is waiting, so . . . get on your way!"

—Dr. Seuss

It's that time again, friends.

Let's clock out, check in, get up, and stretch a bit.

We've done some hard work.

And I just want to stop here and say: **GOOD JOB.**

You have been kicking butt.

You have been strengthening that kindness muscle.

You have been changing the world.

You really have.

But I also want to say: I really hope you've been doing the adventures.

Because let's face it, we've all gotten books like this. We've sat down with the best of intentions.

"This is going to be AMAZING!" we think.

"This is going to CHANGE MY LIFE!"

And then we get busy, because
life is **busy.**

REALLY BUSY.

And it's easy to think that we're just too busy, or too tired, for kindness.

But if we slow down just enough, we discover that we all have time for kindness.

∘ ∘

I was in the middle of filming **The Kindness Diaries** when I found myself in Pittsburgh. I had been looking all day for somewhere to stay the night.

There is no feeling lonelier than being a stranger in a strange town with nowhere to sleep. But I didn't realize how true that was until I met Tony.

Tony was in a park in downtown Pittsburgh when I asked him if I could stay the night with him. So many people had already said no to me that day.

148

I was tired. I was frustrated. I was wondering why I had decided to do this crazy trip in the first place.

Tony was my last hope. He smiled sadly at me and explained,

I would love for you to stay with me, but I don't have a place.

I'm homeless.

AND THEN HE OFFERED,

But if you want to stay with me out here, I can make sure you're safe.

That night, I slept on the streets with Tony. We talked all night. We found out we had a lot in common. We became friends.

But more than that, Tony showed me that no matter how hard or cruel or mean life can be, we can always respond with kindness. If Tony could be kind, then there is no excuse for anyone else not to be. I have never forgotten that lesson.

Tony showed me his life, and he changed mine forever.

I learned that no matter how tired we are, or how busy, the minute we slow down for kindness, we meet someone like Tony. Someone who shows us that true wealth is not in our wallets. It's in our hearts!

And our lives are changed forever.

So, get back in there and pass along the **KINDNESS**.

See what happens when you play cell phone roulette.

See what happens when you get weird and scared and downright silly

and find out what happiness really means.

x x x x x x x x x x x x x x x x x x x x x x x x x x x x x x x x x

Let's check your happiness meter again. Scale of 1-10. Don't think. Just write.

Dr. Seuss was right—you're on your way!

ADVENTURE #13

MUCHAS GRACIAS

GRAZIE! DANKE! MERCI!
THANK YOU!

The really smart writer Anne Lamott says there are only three prayers anyone needs to say:

HELP.
THANKS.
WOW.

"Help" connects us to ourselves.

"Thanks" connects us to other people.

"Wow" connects us to the world.

But I have found that they are all connected to each other.

For today, let's sit in **gracias, danke, merci,** thank you.

Because we all have moments to be grateful for. Recently, I was back on the road for **Kindness Diaries 2** driving through Canada in 30-below weather in a 50-year-old car. I had decided that circumnavigating the globe wasn't enough. I was going to drive from Alaska to Argentina on the kindness of strangers and offer more kindness along the way.

Wow. Great idea, Leon.

Until you crash your 50-year-old car into a snowbank in 30-below weather.

But here is the thing about adventures in kindness: you can find them anywhere.

In school.

At work.

On a plane. Or a train.

Or in a snowbank, with no cell phone reception.

And did I mention it was 30 below?

As I tried to restart my car, I wondered whether my great adventure into kindness was going to end with me frozen in the middle of Canada, but then a car passed. And then that car stopped.

The couple inside immediately pulled my car out of the snow, which was kind enough. But then Colby and Jacquelyn followed me slowly to the next town to make sure I made it there safely. They got out of their car, and we all hugged before they went on their way.

That night, Colby and Jacquelyn showed me that the world is filled with **WOW**.

Sometimes, thank you just doesn't feel like enough.

And sometimes, it's just right.

Like right now.

Today, we're going to say

THANK YOU.

Say thank you to your car before you drive to work or school.

Say thank you to

YOUR SPOUSE,
YOUR TEACHER,
YOUR COWORKERS,
YOUR PARENTS.

Say thank you to

YOUR FRIENDS,

AND SALESPEOPLE,

AND SOMEONE WHO COLD-CALLS YOU RIGHT IN THE MIDDLE OF DINNER.

See how much you have to be grateful for.

See how it **FEELS** when you say

THANK YOU

every second,
   every minute,
      every breath of your day.

If you're 12 years old, **say thank you 12 times.**

If you're 45 years old, **say it 45 times.**

Say it out loud.
   Say it loud.
      Say it so other people can hear you.

Remind them how important it is
to be wowed by the world.

Don't worry if you look like a crazy
person for one day.

(We are all a bit nuts in the end . . .)

Dare yourself to look like a crazy person.

Thank the sun for shining.

Thank the flowers
for blooming.

Thank your brother for being born.

Thank the person in line
with you for their laugh.

Thank everyone who helps
you throughout the day.

Say thank you for the ability
to say thank you . . .

The more we say thank you, the more we feel the WOW.

Because when we say thanks, we not only celebrate other people.

We **see** them.

And they see us.

They stop and say, "You're welcome."

At the end of the day, write how all those thank yous made you feel.

I mean, that is a **lot** of THANK YOU

What do those two little words
mean to you now?

And how do they make you live with
a little more

- -

THANK YOU!

You did it!:

I felt every thank you I gave today. I saw the beauty of the world. I saw its wow. Thanks, Leon, for making me do this today!

(You're welcome.)

ADVENTURE #14

WINNIE LOVE,
PART ONE

Very few people wake up in the morning and say, "How can I break my heart today?"

But kindness requires that we love the world so much, we let our hearts get broken.

Like the great musician Leonard Cohen once said, "There is a crack in everything, that's how the light gets in."

Fifteen years ago, I met my light.

He was a dog named Winston Churchill.

Now Winnie, as I called him (because Winston Churchill is a very formal name for a dog), wasn't just any dog.

Winnie taught me how to love.

Not that I hadn't loved people before (of course I had). But before Winnie, I didn't know what it meant to love someone unconditionally—no matter what mistake they made (or what mess they made on the living room floor). I didn't understand that loving something you know you will ultimately lose will not only crack you right in two, it will also let the light in.

Because what Winnie taught me was that in order to feel unconditional love from others, we first have to give it.

And that's what I did with Winnie.

I gave him so much kindness. I offered him so much patience. I wasn't perfect, but in some ways, my love was. And I remember one day thinking, **Why does this dog bring me so much joy?**

I realized it wasn't about what Winnie was giving me.

It was about what I was giving Winnie.

I thought, What if I treated everyone with the same love
and patience
and tolerance
that I gave to Winnie?

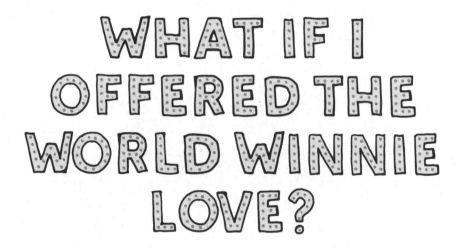

WHAT IF I OFFERED THE WORLD WINNIE LOVE?

Do you have an animal in your life?

Can you borrow one?

Maybe take a trip to your local animal rescue (I said you might adopt a pet).

Or you can go to a local stable or a petting zoo or anywhere that you can spend an hour with an animal. (This is another really fun one if you're a parent and kid doing this together!)

Sit with how that animal makes you feel.

Animals . . .

- LOWER OUR BLOOD PRESSURE
- SOFTEN OUR HEARTS
- CALM OUR SPIRITS
- HELP US HEAL

But most important, they teach us how to let the light in.

It's time again to let your inner child write for you. Remember when we wrote with our nondominant hands?

Well, we're going to do that again.

We're going to write with our hearts (ask your head to take a hike).

WHO ARE FIVE PEOPLE YOU CAN GIVE WINNIE LOVE TO TODAY?

_____

_____

_____

HOW WOULD IT MAKE YOU FEEL?

_____

_____

_____

HOW WOULD IT MAKE YOU HAPPIER?

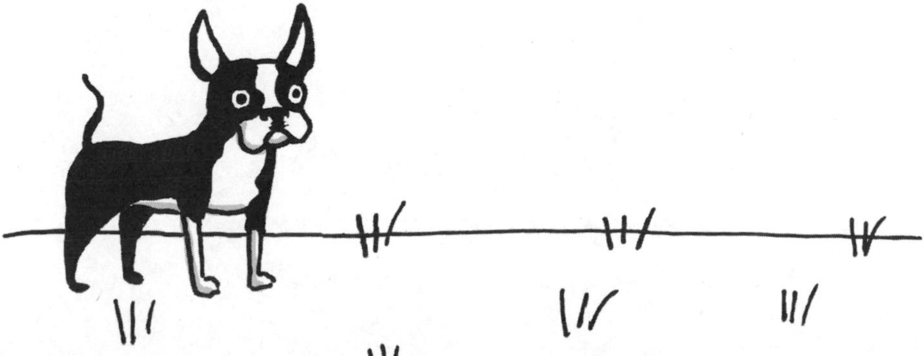

_____

_____

_____

You did it!

Today I realized if I start to love the world like it's a furry dog, I make everything happier—including me.

ADVENTURE #15

WINNIE LOVE,
PART TWO

Three years ago, Winnie died.

They say that dogs are only a part of our lives, but we are all of theirs.

I was all of Winnie's life, and he became a part of mine. He became a part of me, forever. He changed how I saw the world.

Because dogs can't talk (technically), he showed me that the greatest way to communicate was through kindness. It's the only language any of us ever need.

And when he died, it felt like a part of me had died too.

But then I realized that in order to heal my heart I had to begin offering **WINNIE LOVE** every day.

If I couldn't give it to Winnie, I had to give it to others.

Imagine how much our lives would change if we offered everyone we met the same love and affection and patience and generosity we would offer our favorite pet.

WAIT A MINUTE, LEON, HAVE YOU GONE MAD?

Yes, I have. But sometimes being a little mad just means that you're ALIVE.

I started offering Winnie Love not just to my friends and family and coworkers but also to . . .

- **THE PEOPLE I MET AT STARBUCKS.**

- **THE FAMILY IN FRONT OF ME AT THE GROCERY STORE CHECKOUT.**

- **THE WOMAN TAKING TOO LONG TO CROSS THE STREET.**

- **THE HOMELESS MAN ON THE CORNER.**

I realized that kindness was a choice. I **chose** to be kind to Winnie, and I could make the same choice for everyone else in my life—and my world.

You can too.

I wasn't perfect at it. Love is never perfect. Love, especially the unconditional kind, can be pretty messy. And sometimes we aren't very good at it. But it's like any language. The more we use it, the better we get.

The more I wanted to be happy, the more I had to try to practice

 **Kindness**.

By being willing to let the world break my heart, I began to see a whole new beauty in it.

I began to see beauty everywhere around me.

And I'll admit, I began to see it in me too.

So now it's your turn
(you knew that was coming, right?).

It's time to go out into the world and see where you can offer Winnie Love today.

> **Who were those five people that you were going to give Winnie Love to?**

Go do it.

Go out and give those people Winnie Love all day. You don't have to do it perfectly. It can be messy. It can break your heart a little.

But then go beyond them. Give Winnie Love to everyone you meet.

Winnie Love will revolutionize every relationship in your life.

It will offer you more compassion and empathy and patience and kindness and beauty.

It will show you what unconditional love **really** means.

Because we don't feel unconditional love when we are loved unconditionally.

We feel it when we **LOVE** unconditionally.

And once we begin to love our family and our friends and the people we work with and the people we meet at Starbucks and the homeless man on the corner with a love that could break our hearts,

You did it!

☐ I went out into the world and I gave it Winnie Love. It wasn't perfect. It was kind of messy, and it broke my heart a little. But it also filled my life with light, and made the world a little brighter too.

ADVENTURE #16

ANOTHER
SUPER AGENT 007
SECRET MISSION
IMPOSSIBLE THING
THAT YOU CAN
TOTALLY DO

It's that time again. Are you excited?

I am!!

Because there is nothing like going out into the world not knowing what you're going to find.

Every day, we go out into the world. We drive to work. We walk to school. We ride the bus or subway or a bike.

And if someone stopped us and asked, "What are you thinking right now?"

We probably wouldn't be thinking about the world around us.

We would be thinking . . .

I'm running late.

I have so much to do.

I'm tired.

And maybe, every once in a while, we would be thinking,

I'm so excited about the day ahead!

But it's hard to be present in today when you're trapped inside your own head.

Kindness doesn't happen in our brains. I mean, sure, technically it does, yes. But the great, life-changing experience of kindness really only happens when we

CONNECT WITH OUR HEARTS.

When we get out of our own thoughts about running late or having too much to do,

and we can actually stop and see other people.

We realize we're all in this together.

So let's try that today.

Today is an adventure out of our heads and into other people's lives.

Instead of thinking about how late you are (and come on, we're usually all running late at some point. Is it THAT big of a deal?), or the sandwich you left at home, or that you're tired . . .

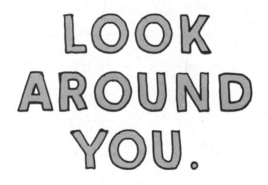

LOOK AROUND YOU.

Next time you're driving to work or walking to school, notice the people around you. Even if they're just sitting in other cars. What do you think they're thinking right now?

And we can all be present in today . . .

once we get out of our own heads

and get into our hearts.

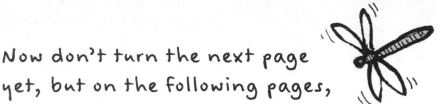

Now don't turn the next page
yet, but on the following pages,
you're going to find four cards.
Each one is going to say something
different. Before you leave the house
today, rip out the four cards. Put them
in your bag. You will need them later.

You can cut the edges to make them
look nice, or you can leave them rough
around the edges.

You can sign them with a personal
message if you want. You can paint
them, decorate them, draw little hearts
if that's your thing.

Kindness does not demand
perfection. In fact, it usually
demands that we be
a little messy.

So back to the cards.

Once you get to work or school or the grocery store or yoga class or the bowling alley—wherever you go today—you're going to go on a **SECRET MISSION**.

You are going to find four people. They are your mission.

Who are you looking for?

You're looking for:

1. Someone who looks like they're running late.

2. Someone who looks like they have too much to do.

3. Someone who looks like they're tired.

4. Someone who looks like they're excited about the day ahead!

IT'S TIME TO USE
YOUR CARDS AND
CONNECT
TO THE PEOPLE
AROUND YOU.

You are an unstoppable force of love and magic who can make all their dreams come true.

#GOBEKIND

f @TheKindnessGuy

🅖 @TheKindnessGuy

You are stronger, more powerful, and more amazing than you think.

#GOBEKIND

f @TheKindnessGuy

@TheKindnessGuy

Thank you for making the world a kinder, happier, more magical place.

#GOBEKIND

f @TheKindnessGuy
@ @TheKindnessGuy

#GOBEKIND

f @TheKindnessGuy

@TheKindnessGuy

After you find your four people,
just go up to them and say . . .

Wait for a moment. Let them look at the
card. Maybe they'll ignore it at first.

But I promise you, they will never forget it.

For those that do read the card . . .

How did their faces change?
What did they say?

How do you think it changed their day?

How did it change yours?

Because that last question shows us the
real treasure.

Once we get out of our **HEADS**, we don't
just get into our **HEARTS**.

We change our **LIVES**.

You did it!

Every time I saw someone read their card, I remembered that we're not meant to be alone. We're all in this together.

ADVENTURE #17

YOU MATTER.

No matter who you are.

No matter where you're from
or how old you are.

No matter how much money you make
or how you're doing in school.

No matter how much you believe in yourself,
doubt yourself,
question who you are.

No matter
what.

YOU
MATTER.

I dare you to put this journal down.
                    Double-dog dare you.

And say those words to yourself.
Out loud.

I MATTER.

You can do better than that.

I MATTER.

Try again.

I MATTER.

Say it as though
your life depends on it.

(You should probably yell that
last one, since it's in bold.)

And you do.
You matter so, so much.

The fact that you are here right now, at this time, on this planet, living and breathing and doing adventures in kindness, is a total miracle of biology and physics and love.

It is scientific proof that you matter. (You're also **made** of matter, so there!)

And if you matter (which I think we have now sufficiently covered),

then so does everyone else living and breathing and walking along this road of life.

That includes the person sitting next to you.

And the person sitting behind you.

And the person who cuts you off in traffic.

And the person who didn't support you at work.

And the person who was mean to you at school.

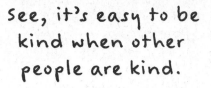

See, it's easy to be kind when other people are kind.

But it's loving people when they're not that's the total game changer.

Think how different the world would be if we responded to every insult with a smile.

There would be no war. There probably wouldn't be Twitter.

Because we matter—
NO MATTER WHAT.

Even if we're being mean or rude or just having a bad day.

So are you ready to do some hard stuff? I think so.

For the rest of the day, be nice when other people aren't.

> Be kind to the person who cuts you off.

> To the cashier who is rude to you.

> To the person you disagree with on Facebook.

> To your child or spouse or mother or father or friend when they say something mean.

Every time someone reacts in anger, offer love.

Because when we show someone else that they matter even when they're being mean or rude or having a bad day, we show them that kindness isn't weakness.

Kindness gives us strength.

But kindness also asks us to be strong.

We all have heard of Nelson Mandela.

For over 27 years, Nelson Mandela was imprisoned because he believed his people should be free. Then he was released. He became president less than two years later.

Did he turn around and punish the people who had imprisoned him?

No. Because Mandela believed that strength meant being kind. It meant forgiveness.

As he once said, "As we let our own light shine, we unconsciously give other people permission to do the same."

He shined his light and the whole world became a brighter place.

We have the chance to do the same when people hurt us.

We show them that they are heard.
Even when they're yelling,
    we are listening.

        We care.

And then watch what happens (I doubt you'll be surprised).

They will drop their anger (maybe),
    their fear (most likely),
        their meanness (probably),
            their bad day (definitely!).

But no matter what, you will remind them that they matter.

YOU MATTER.
I MATTER.
WE MATTER.

And that's all that matters.

You did it!

☐ Today, I found that true strength comes in kindness. When I offered kindness in response to unkindness, I realized just how strong I was.

ADVENTURE #18

SHARE THE MUSIC

I love music.

That doesn't make me special. It just makes me human. I can listen to the same song on repeat forever and forever, over and over. And when I meet someone I care about, one of the first things I do is ask them to listen to my favorite song.

Because if they get that song, they get me.

It's why lovers always have a song. Music is the language of love. It's how we tell our story . . . sometimes without saying a word.

I remember being in Krakow, Poland. I had just visited Auschwitz for the first time, and later in the evening I took a walk around the beautiful Polish city, still overwhelmed by what I had seen. There was an older woman playing the violin on a street corner. She was playing the music from **The Godfather**, but in each movement of her bow I could hear another story. The story of the Holocaust, the catastrophic sadness of mankind.

That is the power of music.

Music touches our hearts because it speaks to who we are underneath the hurt and the sadness and the fear and the pain. Music speaks to our inner worlds.

Do you know there are tribes in Africa who believe that each person has their own song? And that whenever that song is sung, that person is reconnected to their soul. When a person does something wrong, they are not punished. Instead, the tribe sings them their song to remind them who they are. When they get married, their song is sung, and when they have a child, they create a new song for the next generation.

What's your song?

You know the one. The one that feels like it was written for you. That reminds you of who you are.

Yeah, that song. Your soul song.

Got it? Great.

Write it here.

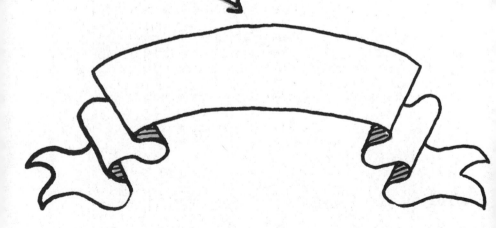

But that's not all. It's time to share your song. To share your inner world.

This can be a scary thing to do, but it also connects us to other people in a way that words cannot. When we share our song, we share our deepest truths. We invite the person we share it with into our inner world. We invite them to see our soul.

You can choose who you want to share your song with. You can call your Kindness Buddy. You can call a friend. But maybe not your best friend. Someone who is about to learn something new about you.

Call them **now**.

SHARE THE SONG.
Tell them Leon made you do it. Tell them why this is your song.
Trust them enough to invite them into your inner world.
Show them a part of your soul.
Let them listen.

ARE THEY LISTENING???

OK, their turn. Ask what their favorite song is. Let them think. They can call you back.

Did they find it?

Perfect.

YOUR TURN TO LISTEN.

What did their song say about them?

Do you love them just a little bit more because of it?

Music is the language of our souls. And when we share music, we share our souls.

We move past our brains and show people. Us. The very essence of
WHO WE ARE.

After you get off the phone, or next time you are home by yourself, put your soul song back on.

AND DANCE TO IT.

Dance like no one is watching.

Dance like everyone is watching

and you just don't care.

You did it!

☐ I found my song, I shared my soul, I danced like the whole world was dancing with me, and you know what, I was happy. Really happy!

ADVENTURE #19

YOU ARE
THE GREATEST OF
ALL TIME

Alright. Time to rip this journal up again.

Literally.

We're yanking out pages.

Why?

Because it's time to be kind to
the most important person in your life.

YOU.

That's right.

Because we
can't reach out
to others until
we can believe
in ourselves.

Legendary boxer Muhammad
Ali once said,

**"I am the greatest,
I said that even
before I knew I was."**

Muhammad Ali was one of the most powerful boxers in history—the greatest of all time. But he was known for his kindness as much as his strength. He was famous for checking in on other boxers after they had taken a beating.

Because as much as Ali loved to talk about how great he was,

he knew saying it doesn't mean anything unless you believe it yourself.

We have given lots of compliments, notes, and kindness to other people.

♥~♥♥~♥♥~♥♥~♥♥~♥♥~♥♥~♥♥~♥♥~♥♥~♥♥

Now we're going to give those same tokens of love to ourselves.

On each of the last five pages of this adventure, you will find a note.

I know they look familiar. That's because the first four are the same notes we handed out to other people.

When we give ourselves the same love
we give to others,
   we realize how much we can change
   people's lives—including our own.

The fifth card is blank.

Rip them out of your journal.

Again, you can do whatever you want
with them:

   You can cut the edges.

   You can color them in.

      You can write yourself
      a message.

   You can even eat them
   (OK, don't eat them!).

But on the last one, you will definitely
need to write yourself a message.

Think of the best compliment you can give yourself.

Be brave.

Believe in yourself.

See how remarkable you are

and always have been.

If there is one thing you absolutely wished someone had told you about yourself write it here.

Here's mine:

Leon—you deserve to be in love genuinely, deeply, forever, with someone who loves to connect with the world in the same way you do.

Now it's your turn.

You can go back to your childhood or to yesterday.

Tell yourself the words you have been waiting to hear.

Write them now.

Once you're ready, go get your tape.

> (Remember when I said you would need tape?)

Now post them throughout your home.

In your bathroom.

On your alarm clock.

On your refrigerator.

On the inside of your front door.

Wherever you will see them in the morning before you start your day.

You can even take one to work or to school.

You can put one in your car or your purse or wallet.

You can hide one in your coat pocket and pull it out throughout the day.

Because when we believe in ourselves,

we can truly believe in others.

♥ ♥

Leave your notes up around your house.

How do they make you feel every day?

How do they change your life?

You are stronger, more powerful, and more amazing than you think.

Thank you for making
the world a kinder, happier,
more magical place.

I've got your back, friend. We're all in this together.

I learned how to believe in myself so I could believe in other people. And those silly notes are my reminder every day that in order to be happy, I have to be kind and gentle to ME!

REALLY QUICK, SUPER IMPORTANT, INCREDIBLY MOTIVATIONAL STORY ABOUT KINDNESS

"If we have no peace, it is because we have forgotten that we belong to each other."

—Mother Teresa

We think as long as we look good on the outside, it doesn't matter how our insides feel.

But kindness starts on the inside.

When I first set out on my original round-the-world journey, I thought I was rebelling against everything I had been told to want—

the desk job,

the successful life,

COMMITMENT.

But the more time I spent out on the road, the more I started to wonder: Was I rebelling against those things or was I just running from them?

When I was a kid, I couldn't wait to get out of school at the end of the day. I would run through the front doors as though the building was on fire (sometimes I wished it was). But then home wasn't much easier, and once I got there, all I wanted to do was leave. I was only happy in that place in between.

Later, when I became a grown-up (if that's what you would call me!), I found my home out on the road. But every time I left for an adventure, part of me wanted to go back to my real home. Once I was home, I wanted to leave again.

And then I found myself in Calcutta, India. The home of Mother Teresa.

I mean, I'm pretty sure it goes without saying that Mother Teresa had the market cornered on kindness. But she knew that kindness took work. While in Calcutta, I found myself in the convent where she used to live, which is now dedicated to her. I saw the room where she slept, her clothes and sandals laid out. And downstairs, in the middle of the main room, sat her quiet and simple tomb.

In that stillness, I remembered that great quote from her about belonging . . .

"IF WE HAVE NO PEACE, IT IS BECAUSE WE HAVE FORGOTTEN THAT WE BELONG TO EACH OTHER."

I realized that my adventures in kindness, whether at home or in

Calcutta, weren't about rebelling, nor were they about RUNNING.

They were about connecting with other people.

If I wanted to find peace in both places, I had to find a way to BELONG.

Belonging not just to the great adventures of the world but also to my home.

MY PEACE BEGINS AT HOME. MY PEACE BEGINS WITH ME.

As does my Kindness.
As does yours.

These adventures aren't just about having fun, though I hope you've had a lot. In fact, I **insist** you do—or you might as well throw this journal away right now!

(Hey, hey, not so fast.
That's your BFF, remember!)

These adventures are also about finding **peace** . . .

IN YOUR HOME,
ON THE ROAD,
AND IN THE HEART OF
THE ONE AND ONLY,
ABSOLUTELY AMAZING YOU.

So let's do this. Pull out your happiness meter. 1–10.

No judgment. No matter what your number is, know that you belong.

ADVENTURE #20

#GOBEKIND

This isn't a long adventure because it doesn't take a lot these days to share your love with the world. We are more connected than ever. But we can't experience the depth of that connection until we make kindness our favorite app.

Are you ready to take kindness viral? Great!

All you have to do is go onto social media and say something kind about someone.

x x x x x x x x x x x x x x x x x x x x x x x x

And then tag five people to do the same thing.

It's that simple.

#GOBEKIND

Today I spread kindness and a little bit of magic on social media. I didn't fight with strangers, I didn't argue. I just brought some love to the party, and watched it grow. And I grew too . . .

ADVENTURE #21

_____

IT'S A SMALL
WORLD . . . AFTER ALL

_____

It's time to get back out there.

To get to know
THE WORLD AROUND YOU.

It's gonna be a biggie. It's gonna take bravery. It's gonna make the world a better place.

-◎

We live on a planet with more than 200 countries and over 7,000 languages.

Some of us are men, some are women, some don't identify as one or the other.
Some of us have more money.
Some of us have less of it.
Some of us pray to different gods.
Some of us don't pray at all.

And yet we all walk the earth next to one another.

We breathe the same air.
We smile the same way.
We cry the same way too.

It's like the great Muhammad Ali once said:

Me. We.

When we turn on the morning news, all we hear is how different we are.

We argue.

We fight.

We go to war.

Not because we are bad people

but because we have forgotten how much
WE ARE THE SAME.

Made up of the same

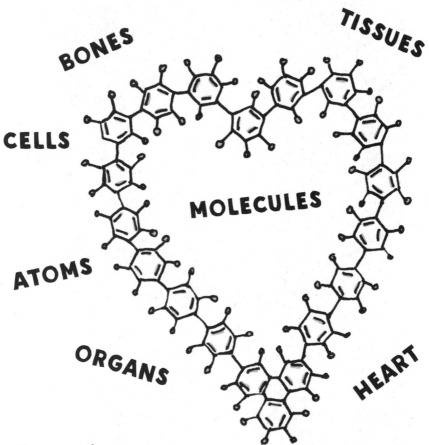

BONES

TISSUES

CELLS

MOLECULES

ATOMS

ORGANS

HEART

You and me
and everyone else.

On the inside, **WE ARE IDENTICAL.**

So now it's time to find one person who is different from you.

They could be

- ● WHITE
- ● BLACK
- ● POOR
- ● RICH
- ● CHRISTIAN
- ● JEWISH
- ● MUSLIM

They could be at work. At school. In the street.

Tell them you are doing an adventure in kindness

and invite them to lunch or coffee or (if you're old enough) even a beer at the pub.

You might get turned down a few times. It might feel weird. It might get awkward.

But if you don't succeed with the first person, ask two more.

I promise you will find one by the third try.

If you breathe in deep, take a pause, and use your intuition,

you will find your new friend.

I once had to ask total strangers if I could board their ship to cross an ocean.

Asking someone out to coffee is nothing.

From there, I can't tell you what will happen.

I can't explain to you the mystery of two humans connecting.

How when we sit down across from each other

all the fears

and the differences

and the otherness

and the not knowing

turn into the deepest of knowing.

Because when we truly SEE each other, we find out that we are THE SAME.

_____

When you get home, describe your new friend.

Don't look at how they're different from you.

Write down all the ways in which you are similar.

Maybe write a little story.
Maybe draw a picture.

How does the world feel like a smaller place?

You just made that happen!

☐ I connected with a stranger and suddenly the whole world felt a little smaller. ☺ I felt like I was a part of the world. It is a small world after all!

ADVENTURE #22

KINDNESS IS COOL

Being cool means something different to everyone.

I used to think being cool meant how many famous people I knew (which was none, so I wasn't very cool at all). I used to think cool was how many people liked me (thankfully, I was a little better at that than collecting famous friends). Or the cool car I was driving or the cool parties I attended or the cool places I visited (and I'll be honest, I've gone to a lot of cool places).

But then I realized being cool is lot simpler than that.

It means being so

HONEST
AND **BRAVE**
AND CREATIVE
AND AUTHENTIC

that you don't need to be anything else but KIND.

Like Muhammad Ali (him again!) believed,

"Service to others is the rent you pay for your room here on earth."

I mean, how **COOL** is that?

We all know people who are able to do this.

They are kind

  because they are confident.

CONFIDENCE
CREATES
KINDNESS CREATES
CONFIDENCE
CREATES KINDNESS.

Say that ten times real fast. OK, you don't have to . . .

So maybe it's time we start becoming fans of people who aren't just cool.

Maybe we need to create fan clubs for people who are **KIND**.

So instead of thinking of actors or soccer players or Justin Bieber when you think of cool,

think of someone who is changing one life.

That means someone who is changing the world.

It's time to write a fan letter.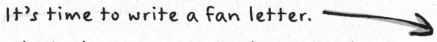

Who is the one person in the world who you think most makes being **KIND** look **COOL**?

Or if you want, you can send them an email,
a tweet,
a DM.

Tell them how they are changing the world.
Share how they are inspiring you to do the same.

When we start honoring people for being

HONEST
BRAVE
CREATIVE
AUTHENTIC

we make kindness cool again.

(Guess what? It always was.)

Dear —————,

Your fan,

You did it!

☐ Kindness really does change everything! It is changing the way I think about peace and happiness and love and belonging . . . and what it means to be cool. And I wrote a fan letter today! I wonder if they will write back??

ADVENTURE #23

THE KIND OF
SECRET MISSION
THAT EVERYONE
KNOWS ABOUT

We're going on another mission.

It will be filled with laughter
    and tears
        and inspiration
            and mind-blowing realizations.

It will take you on adventures unknown
(like on a broken-down motorcycle across
the world).

We are
going to . . .

**YOUR
HOUSE!!!!**

That's right. Because some adventures
don't require approaching strangers
on the street or taking people out to
lunch. Some adventures take place in
our imagination.

Because tonight is
MOVIE NIGHT.

But not just any movie night.

The kind that when the credits roll, you feel like the movie has just begun.

The kind that stays with you for days, weeks, years.

The kind that just might **CHANGE YOUR LIFE.**

Ever since I was a little kid, I have lost myself in movies.

Within the space of two hours, I would take a trip into someone else's life. I would get to see places I had never been before. The music would soar, and the camera would zoom out over

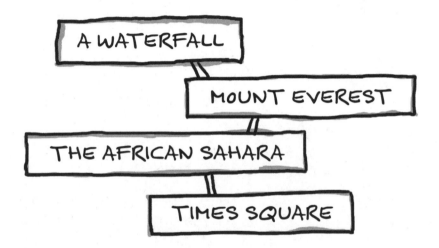

A WATERFALL

MOUNT EVEREST

THE AFRICAN SAHARA

TIMES SQUARE

and I would feel like I was a part of the world.

I wouldn't feel alone.

And I didn't even have to leave my house (though I do strongly suggest leaving the house).

Remember when I said that years ago
I saw the movie **The Motorcycle Diaries**
and it changed my entire life?

That is how powerful a movie can be.

It can lift us from our seats,
    from our boredom,
        from our comfort zone,
and show us the lives we were meant to live.

-◉

So now it's your turn.

Because tonight you get to choose:

WHICH LIFE-CHANGING MOVIE DO YOU WANT TO WATCH?

Choose wisely.

Here are six movies that show how one kind person can **CHANGE A LIFE**.

How one kind person can **CHANGE THE WORLD**.

<u>Moonlight</u>

<u>Life Is Beautiful</u>

<u>The Pursuit of Happyness</u>

<u>Forrest Gump</u>

<u>Dead Poets Society</u>

<u>The Motorcycle Diaries</u>

Invite your Kindness Buddy over.
Watch with your friends or family.
Spend a quiet evening at home alone.

But immerse yourself in the movie.
Experience someone else's heartbreak.

See that you're **NOT ALONE**.

When the credits rolled,
   did you feel like the movie had
   just begun?

That's because it has.

-⊚

Now it's your turn to go on that
great adventure.

Choose whichever one or however many of
these adventures you want in your life:

- Be who you truly are.
- Make someone laugh.
- Help someone in need.
- Find a park bench and chat
  with some strangers.
- Pursue your dreams.
- Get a rusty motorbike like
  Che Guevara and Leon Logothetis
  and cross the world. (Don't worry—
  there's more than enough room out
  there on the road for both of us.)

You won't be able to do any of these things overnight (or even watch all these movies). But you can start them right now.

Like Robin Williams said in **Dead Poets Society,**

"CARPE DIEM. SEIZE THE DAY."

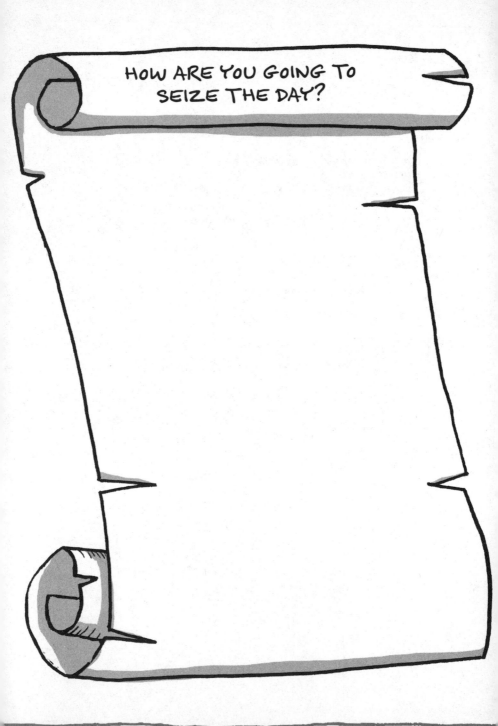

You did it!

☐ I watched the movie of my dreams tonight. I decided to go out and live it. And my life felt different.

ADVENTURE #24

UNPLUG YOURSELF!

You know it's gonna be a tough one if we saved it for **Adventure #24.**

WHAT DO YOU MEAN, LEON?

Look, I get why you're suspicious.

I know what I am about to ask won't be easy.

But I am still going to ask you to do it.

And I can only hope you'll put away all your no's and say

YES.

I am going to ask you to go a day without your phone.

I know there are a million reasons why you can't do it (#workschoolfriends-planskidsemergenciesFacebookInstagram-OhMyGodWhatAmIGoingToDoWithMyself).

I understand. But friends, this is something we must do.

BECAUSE WHEN WE UNPLUG FROM OUR PHONES, WE HAVE NO CHOICE BUT TO CONNECT TO THE WORLD.

And when we connect, we get a chance to be kind. We get a chance to reach out to complete strangers. We get to know them. We get to know **ourselves**.

A couple of years ago, I was in Los Angeles at one of those outdoor shopping malls when all the power went out. Suddenly, everyone was disconnected from their phone networks. Digitally, we were stranded.

But what we quickly realized was
WE HAD EACH OTHER.

Now is our chance to have each other again. But first we have to disconnect.

Hello?
You still there?

I get that you might need to wait until the weekend for this.

Or if you can, at work, just use your computer, and not your phone.

But we're taking a break from the great distraction that is our phones

and we're going to remember what it's like to just **be**.

It's not that big of a deal when you think about it.

Remember what it was like when we weren't checking our phones every five minutes?

Remember when we were at a party where we didn't know anyone, and we actually had to **talk** to people?

If you were born after these times, I promise you—it was crazy.

We didn't have the internet. We could only connect to one another.

Imagine all the time and energy and attention we'd have if we weren't looking at Facebook and Instagram and Twitter and our emails

Well, for one day, we're going to go back there.

It will be like stepping into a time machine to 2005.

We'll have flip phones and post things on MySpace.

But I'll warn you right now:

For one day, everything will feel different.

Because without your phone, you will be forced to **connect**. You'll probably realize it makes you a little happier too.

> In fact, studies show the more you use your phone, the less happy you are.

Because though we might all belong to Facebook, we have stopped belonging to each other.

When we put down our phones, we enter into a deeper relationship with the world.

- With our friends.
- With our family.
- With the stranger standing next to us at the grocery store or in line for the bus.
- With the person sitting next to us at Starbucks, or stranded with us in the middle of a power outage in LA.

So before you pick up that phone again at the end of the day . . .

Stop yourself. Check in.

HOW DID IT FEEEEEEEEEL?

What does it look like for your relationships,

for every interaction in your life,

if you do it without your phone in hand?

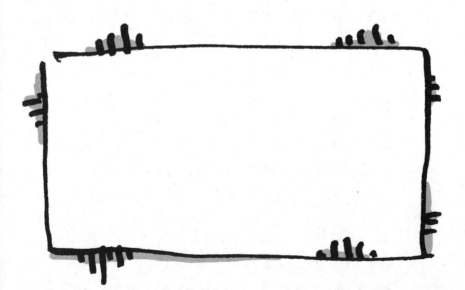

I'll tell you a little secret. I don't use a smartphone. And do you know why?

Because it takes me away from life.

My friends make fun of my flip phone, but the truth is, it keeps me right here, with you.

What does staying right here feel like for you?

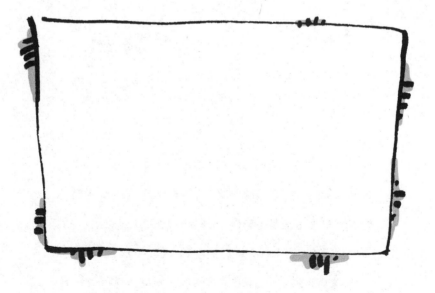

Today, I went into a time
machine—back when I didn't
have Facebook, Instagram,
Twitter, SnapChat, Google.
Instead, I just had me. And you.
And we were in this together.

ADVENTURE #25

NOW WE TALK
TO THAT TREE

Way smarter people than
me have been talking for a
long time about how nature
changes us.

People like Albert Einstein
(OK, so people way, way, way
smarter than me), who said,

Because nature reflects the best of this world to us.

It shows us who we are,
   where we came from,
      and that we all SHARE THE EARTH in the same way.

No matter who we are or what we do or what we think.

Most of us grew up staring up at the sky.
   Running through the grass.
      Climbing trees.
      Splashing in the ocean.

We all have our own definition of God, but you can't help but look out at the horizon, look up at the vastness of the stars, see the flower growing between the cracks in cement,

         and not feel the presence of
         the universe's great force.

IT REMINDS US HOW SMALL WE ALL ARE
YET HOW VERY, VERY IMPORTANT.

And perhaps more than anything,

NATURE CONNECTS US TO EACH OTHER.

But first we must be connected to nature.

Today, we are going to **CONNECT**.

Make some time for yourself to spend outside.

If you live near the ocean, head to the beach.

If you live near the mountains, go for a hike.

Look up at the stars and feel how absolutely miraculous this world we share is.

Talk to a tree.

No, really.

Talk to a tree.

Or to the sea.

Or to the sky.

Spend the day in nature and see how it makes you love the world a little more.

See how it fills your heart with happiness.

Years ago, I got to drive through New Zealand. I remember seeing these perfect mountains rising up into the sky. I pulled my car over and got out. They were so perfect that they looked like they had been Photoshopped.

And I realized that if the universe could make that, if the universe was able to create such perfection, then it couldn't have done too bad of a job with me. Or you. The same expert that made the world—from stardust to mountaintops—made you too, and when you connect with nature, you are reminded of that. You are reminded of your own amazing place in the world.

When we connect with nature,
WE CONNECT WITH EACH OTHER.

And when we connect with each other,
WE UNDERSTAND ONE ANOTHER BETTER.

We understand everything better.

Shameless plug: if anyone from the New Zealand tourism board is reading this, please contact me. I would like a job!

☐ I spent time in nature and I saw myself. And guess what? I am made of stardust and mountaintops!

REALLY QUICK, SUPER IMPORTANT, INCREDIBLY MOTIVATIONAL STORY ABOUT KINDNESS

> "Barbecue may not be the road to world peace, but it's a start."
>
> —Anthony Bourdain

Every day, it feels like the world is engaged in one really big family argument. No one can agree on anything, and our disagreements are all out in the open for everyone to see.

It's not easy sometimes to be kind in a world that can feel so cruel. But sometimes, when the world is cruel, it's actually offering us an amazing opportunity to be kind.

It's asking us to create communities around **Kindness**.

And Anthony Bourdain was right. Sometimes all it takes is a **BARBECUE**.

I was in Canada on my latest adventure when I met a man named Richard in Red Deer, Alberta. Richard is a travel agent. But he is also much more than that. Once a week, Richard hosts a barbecue at his house.

SO WHAT, LEON? LOTS OF PEOPLE HAVE BARBECUES.

Yes, but Richard doesn't just invite his friends and family. He invites refugees from all over the world who have just arrived in Red Deer. People from Syria, Somalia, Angola, Afghanistan. The whole world comes to his house.

And they bring food. And drinks and beer. They laugh. And share their stories. They share their lives. They have created a **community of kindness**. And they are building the road to world peace, one plate of barbecue at a time.

I was invited to one of these amazing parties, and it was like being in the middle of the UN. Except with way more laughing ... and beer. Not a lot of beer at the UN.

I looked around at all those people and realized: This is who we are. We belong to each other.

Because when people come together, when they find their common ground, when they toss aside their differences and fire up the grill, we discover a really simple fact:

WHEN WE ARE IN COMMUNITY, WE ARE HAPPY.

By creating community, we create happiness.

And yes, I do believe that happiness is what will bring us world peace.

Or at least peace in our own hearts.

So take a breath.

Right now. Take a deep and powerful inhale.

And then let it all go.

Let go of all the **DIFFERENCES**.

Let go of your **FEARS** and **FAILINGS**.

Let go of feeling bad that maybe you didn't complete every adventure in the book.

Maybe you just read some of them.

Maybe you could even work on doing some of those adventures right now.

You are building your own yellow brick road—and it might lead to Oz, or it might lead you right back home.

Who knows? It might lead to **WORLD PEACE**.

Sure, you can skip a few bricks, but the more you miss, the harder it will be to find your way.

ADVENTURE #26

PAIN CREATES
COMMUNITY

It's time to share your big hurt.

It's time to find other people who hurt like you do.

When we share our pain, we don't only change the world—
    we change who we are.

Brain scientist Daniel Siegel says the only way to change the brain

is to connect with another human.

It's how we
heal ourselves.

    It's how we **heal our world.**

In the last few weeks of my latest journey, driving from Alaska to Argentina in a 50-year-old busted yellow Beetle, I found myself in Ecuador. I was exhausted. I had been dealing with my 50-year-old Beetle breaking down all over North America, Central America, and now South America. I had been dealing with bandits. With bug bites. With confusing maps.

And it was just too much.

Sometimes kindness can feel like that. Like we are giving but getting nothing in return.

But then we offer the one thing we all have, but are afraid to give.

WE SHARE OUR PAIN.

I met some people along the road, and I finally shared my pain with them.

One of the people I met that day was a woman who worked for a dog rescue. She had been working in an office, and then one morning, she woke up (a lot like me) and said, **I can't do this anymore**. She gave up her career, her old dreams, and opened up a rescue to take care of animals that other people had thrown away. As she said, "I decided that love was more important than a desk."

When I found out about the dog rescue, I began to tell her about Winnie. And then I broke. I just couldn't hold in the grief of losing my best friend and the exhaustion of the road anymore. But then the tears changed. I wasn't sad.

I was happy.

IN SHARING MY PAIN, I HAD RELEASED IT.

It is time to share your big hurt . . . and find your big happy.

It might be scary. It might be embarrassing.

But remember—we've redefined **COOL**.

Being brave is cool.

Being brave helps us to be happy.

- -

So go back to that **BIG HURT** you wrote down in **Adventure #5**.

It's up to you who you want to share it with.

It can be your Kindness Buddy.
It can be a group of friends.
It can be on social media.

When we share our big hurt,
we build community through our
shared pain.

How will you share yours?

Sharing your pain is just about the coolest thing you can do.

And the bravest.

It will not only free you from the big hurt—
it will help you find the people who
can help you heal.

And then—who knows? You might help
them to **HEAL** too.

In fact, I promise that you will.

You did it!

☐ I shared my biggest
hurt, and I found people who
understood. I found out that by
sharing my hurt, I was sharing
my heart.

ADVENTURE #27

CREATE YOUR OWN
ADVENTURE

Now it's your turn to be Leon. No, you don't need to drive from Alaska to Argentina in a 50-year-old yellow Beetle. But you do get to . . .

CREATE YOUR OWN KINDNESS ADVENTURE.

That's right. Figure out one choice you could make, one action or activity that you could do, that would create more kindness in the world. That would make you happy.

You can take a friend roller skating. You can buy flowers for a stranger. You can create a small or big adventure with your kids, your parents, someone else you love. Or maybe someone you've just met.

Remember how, when I was a kid, one teacher taught me such a big lesson in kindness that it changed the entire direction of my life? Mrs. Mann is the reason I wanted to spread kindness. When we inspire others to be kind, the world becomes a kinder place.

ARE YOU READY TO SPREAD THE KINDNESS?

What's your ADVENTURE?

There's room—have fun!

And now it's time to share it. Post your adventure to social media. Invite five friends to create their own kindness adventure. Think of it as the next ice bucket challenge. Except this one is the **#gobekind** challenge.

See how many of your friends do it— and then ask them to share their own kindness adventures with the world!

Each of us is a butterfly, and we are starting a revolution by flapping our wings of kindness. They're going to feel it on the other side of the world. I promise.

All we have to do is

GO BE KIND.

Right now.

You did it!

☐ I started to spread the kindness, and I found out that I'm not the only butterfly. I think I'm ready, Leon. It's time to change the world.

(Don't worry, friend. That's just what we're about to do!)

ADVENTURE #28

CHANGE ONE LIFE

You made it!

THE BIG KAHUNA.

This is your final big adventure.

You know how I keep saying all you have to do is **CHANGE ONE LIFE TO CHANGE THE WORLD**?

Well, it's true. You know how I know?

Because when I was 16, one small act of kindness changed my life.

That one small act saved it.

In high school, I ate lunch by myself in the library every day for two years. I would lose myself in books so I could avoid other people.

I was tired of being bullied. I was tired of NOT BEING SEEN.

And one day, I began to wonder whether it might be easier if I just wasn't here at all.

Then a boy walked up to my table.
I had seen him around school, but we
weren't friends.

I didn't even look up. I thought he was just
going to make fun of me for sitting alone
because that's what everyone else did.

But he didn't. Instead,
he asked,

DO YOU WANT TO
COME AND EAT LUNCH WITH
ME AND MY FRIENDS?

I thought it was a
joke at first. But then he
smiled, the kind of smile you
know is genuine, and he said,

REALLY, LEON.
COME AND SIT
WITH US.

PLEASE.

I was scared to say yes, but
what that boy had just done
was so absolutely brave,
I wanted to be brave too.

And I joined him and his friends for lunch.

Those boys became my friends. And that one act changed my life forever.

Now it's your chance to do the same thing.

Because it's time to find someone who needs a friend.

- Maybe they're sitting by themselves at school or at Starbucks.
- Maybe they're crying outside a church.
- Maybe they're sitting at a park.
- Maybe they're sitting in your living room.

Life can be hard

and some days can be harder for some people than for others.

So find that person who looks like they could use a friend.

I don't mean someone who needs to get their refrigerator moved.

I mean someone who is in pain,

someone who is stuck,

someone who is hurt.

Reach out to them and see how you can help them get whatever they need.

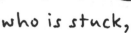

Maybe they need one small gift that would forever change the course of their life.

Maybe they just need a friend.

When we look around at the people we love, the people we barely know, it shouldn't be too hard to find one person who needs

SOMETHING.

When I went around the world, I offered gifts large and small.

Sometimes it was helping people **RECONNECT** with each other.

Sometimes it was helping people **RECONNECT** with themselves.

So who is your person?

Enough talking.
Enough writing.
Enough thinking.
GO TO THEM.

Ask them what they **NEED**.
And then really listen to them. Read between the lines.

Then give them that **GIFT**.

You never know how one act of kindness might forever change someone's life.

When you get home, call your Kindness Buddy.

Tell them what you've done.
See if they might be willing to do the same.

Now.
Imagine if we all did that every day.

CHANGED SOMEONE'S LIFE AND THEN INSPIRED A FRIEND TO DO THE SAME.

Imagine how different our world would be.

Guess what? You're doing it—you're changing the world. **EVERY DAY**.

Just by **BEING KIND**.

You did it!

I just laid the last brick on my road to happiness. I just connected with someone in such a powerful way that both of our lives were changed forever. And I think, just maybe, the world was changed too.

ADVENTURE #28½

THE END (ALMOST)

This mission is mine.

Do you see the postcard at the end of the book?

Yeah, that one.

Well, your only job here is to fill it out.

As you can see, it has a very simple question on it:

How did you make someone feel less Alone?

Go ahead, be honest.

Let me know how you changed someone's life.

Let me know how you just changed the world.

For every card I receive, I will donate a book to a child in need. I will share your kindness with the ones who need it most.

When I was a kid, books were my best friends. They showed me worlds I had never seen. They were also my only friends (that's why I ate lunch in the library).

They showed me that I wasn't alone.

And now, because of you, another kid will get that life-changing gift.

We'll give it to them together.

And then who knows what will happen?

————————

That's the amazing thing about these adventures into kindness we've taken together.

THEY'RE NOT OVER.

Not even close.

It's like when you think the credits are almost finished . . .
   and then the movie's bloopers begin
   to play.

Because some of the best parts of

GO BE KIND start after
you think the adventures have ended.

The biggest surprise:

YOU AND I ARE JUST GETTING STARTED.

We're going to go out every day and find adventures in kindness,

and we're going to keep sharing about them.

Until everyone begins to realize that, in the end,

is the only thing that will heal us.

Together, we are going to **GO BE KIND.**

Together, we're going to change lives (that's a promise).

Together, we are going to change the world.

Edit: **WE ALREADY HAVE.**

xxxxxxxxxxxxxxxxxxxxxxxxxxxxxxxxxxxxxx

We did it!

☑ Don't worry—I'll take care of this one.

ACKNOWLEDGMENTS

I am deeply grateful for the privilege of sharing my heart with the world. For without all the people I have gotten to meet on life's road (and that includes you the reader), there would be no books, no shows, and no speeches.

I owe a debt of gratitude to many, but here I will mention a few . . .

Mrs. Mann: Without your kindness, there would be no **Go Be Kind** movement. Without your kindness there would be no me. Truth. Thank you for all you did all those years ago; I have made it my mission in life to give to others what you gave to me: love.

Ted (the wisest man I know): Your love and kindness has changed who I am on a profound level. You have saved me more times than you will ever know. I love you.

Ramchandra: Your wisdom keeps me going in times of struggle. Thank you.

Steve and Nacho: You will forever be in my heart. Your friendship means more to me than I can explain in words.

The team at BenBella Books: Thank you for believing in my mission and my desire to light up the world one kind act at a time. You have given me the platform to share my soul with the world and I am deeply grateful.

Coleen: Thank you for believing in me and enabling me to sail smoothly through publishing's wide seas.

Suzanne: You have a heart of gold and a deep and an enduring wisdom. I wouldn't be where I am today if it wasn't for all the times I have sat on your couch and poured out my pain and joy. You see me and for that I am deeply grateful.

Kristen: Once again, without you, we wouldn't be here! Your magic sprinkles are truly rather magnificent. And one day, in the not-so-distant future, I will be the one coming to one of your book signings! May the light always be there when you need it, bro.

Michael: You made this book come alive. You are a master and a maestro. Godspeed, brother.

Isabella: You are a special human and I appreciate the relationship we have. May it last for many decades to come. Thank you for your feedback on this journal. :)

My family: As we always say, "One for all and all for one."

Last but not least, to the great **Winston**, the naughtiest dog in England! You are gone, but my dearest of friends, you are not forgotten. You taught me so much.

ABOUT THE AUTHOR

LEON LOGOTHETIS is a global adventurer, motivational speaker, and philanthropist. **It wasn't always that way.** He used to be a broker in the city of London where he felt uninspired and chronically depressed. He gave it all up for a life on the road. This radical life change was inspired by the inspirational movie **The Motorcycle Diaries.**

The days of living and working behind his "slab of wood" (or desk, to the layman) are well and truly over. His new passion: Finding ways for your **inner rebel** (that voice that tells you that you are worth so much more than you think) to come out and play.

Leon has visited nearly 100 countries and traveled to every continent. He is the star of the Netflix series **The Kindness Diaries I,** where he circumnavigates the globe, relying on the kindness of strangers, while giving life-changing gifts along the way.

Currently, he is starring in **The Kindness Diaries 2**, traveling from Alaska to Argentina in a 50-year-old Beetle, and discovering kindness north and south of the equator.

Prior to **The Kindness Diaries**, Leon was the host of the TV series **Amazing Adventures of a Nobody**, which was broadcast across the world by National Geographic International and, over the course of three seasons, saw Leon cross America, the United Kingdom, and Europe on just 5 dollars, 5 pounds, and 5 euros a day, respectively.

Leon is no stranger to adventure. He teamed up with First Book and drove a car from London to Mongolia, raising money to buy 10,000 books for

underprivileged children in America.
He also drove a vintage London taxi
across America, giving free cab rides to
the needy and working with Classwish
to bring hope back to the schools
of America.

Leon has documented his travels for
numerous media outlets including CBS This
Morning, **Good Morning America**, CNN,
Los Angeles Times, **San Francisco Chronicle**,
Outside, **Huffington Post**, **Psychology
Today**, and the **New York Times**. He is the
author of three bestselling books, **Amazing
Adventures of a Nobody**, **The Kindness
Diaries**, and **Live, Love, Explore**. He lives in
Los Angeles.

I HELPED SOMEONE FEEL LESS ALONE TODAY

#gobekind

f @ @TheKindnessGuy

Read Adventure 28½, and then follow these steps:

---

1. Tear out and trim the bottom of this postcard.

2. Tell me how you changed someone's life.

3. Put a stamp on it and mail it to me!

4. For every postcard I receive, I will donate a book to a child in need.

DEAR LEON,

I did my homework by:

Leon Logothetis
P.O. Box 46232
Los Angeles, CA 90046

THE KINDNESS DIARIES   Now streaming on NETFLIX